ANTHROPOLOGICAL PAPERS

MUSEUM OF ANTHROPOLOGY, UNIVERSITY OF MICHIGAN

NO. 56

ARCHAEOLOGY AND CERAMICS AT THE MARKSVILLE SITE

BY

ALAN TOTH

ANN ARBOR

THE UNIVERSITY OF MICHIGAN, 1974

ISBN (print): 978-0-932206-54-1
ISBN (ebook): 978-1-951519-15-5

Browse all of our books at
sites.lsa.umich.edu/archaeology-books.

Order our books from the University of Michigan
Press at www.press.umich.edu.

For permissions, questions, or manuscript queries,
contact Museum publications by email at umma-
pubs@umich.edu or visit the Museum website at
lsa.umich.edu/ummaa.

ACKNOWLEDGEMENTS

In the course of writing a report on archaeological materials collected a generation ago and now housed in institutions dispersed throughout the United States, one becomes greatly indebted to many people. I would like especially to thank the following people and institutions, without whom this paper could not have been written: Philip Phillips and James B. Griffin for their pioneer work on the subject and indirect guidance throughout the research; Stephen Williams and Jeffrey Brain for their critical reading of the rough draft and many useful suggestions; Robert Neuman for his assistance in assembling the necessary research materials and critical reading of the manuscript; Robert S. Neitzel for supplying many firsthand observations pertaining to the 1939 excavations; Marvin Graham, Supervisor of the Marksville Museum, for permitting access to materials on display; the Smithsonian Institution for the loan of collections and negatives from the U.S. National Museum of Natural History; and the New Orleans *Times-Picayune* for permission to quote the 1851 description of the Marksville site in its entirety. The present study is a revised version of a masters' thesis submitted to Louisiana State University, and therefore I add my thanks for their direction to the members of my committee: William G. Haag, Jay Edwards and Sherwood Gagliano.

Since the final manuscript was submitted for publication, I have had the opportunity to examine additional collections from Marksville and related sites. For access to the new material, I am especially indebted to William Fitzhugh and George Phebus of the Smithsonian Institution and to L. B. Jones of Minter City, Mississippi. The recently acquired information does supplement the primary analysis, but existing conclusions are not affected. The new data are incorporated in the footnotes which update the original study.

This project is part of the long term program of research by the Lower Mississippi Survey, Peabody Museum, Harvard University. The publication of this paper is partially supported by the Survey.

TABLE OF CONTENTS

LIST OF TABLES

LIST OF FIGURES

INTRODUCTION

THE literature on American archaeology is replete with references to the Marksville site (16 Av 1) in Avoyelles Parish, Louisiana. In fact, virtually every attempt to speculate on the external connections of a Hopewell, or Hopewellian-influenced, site anywhere in the eastern United States pays lip service to Marksville at some juncture. For most researchers, unfortunately, there is a very slim body of hard data—all of 1930s vintage—with which to work, and, despite increased archaeological activity in the Lower Mississippi Valley since World War II, little or nothing new has been written on the Marksville site. It is not surprising, therefore, to find a number of misconceptions about Marksville and the material evidence which was unearthed at the site.

One does not have to look hard to find examples of ill-founded notions about Marksville: the bird design vessels at the site are alleged to be northern importations (Prufer, 1964:76); the ceremonial earthworks are nonchalantly identified with the Marksville phase by the most uncompromising scholars (see, for example, Sears, 1964:265 and Willey, 1966:291) although there is absolutely no evidence pertaining to their date; maize and squash are traced to Marksville (Struever and Vickery, 1973) with no indication of the highly ambiguous circumstances surrounding the find. In short, there is a genuine need for more sound information on Marksville and, in view of the increasing concern with models such as the Hopewell Interaction Sphere, that information must be given the widest possible dissemination before additional fallacies or uncertainties become ingrained in the literature.

The explicit goal of this paper is to begin the task of collating and assessing the hard evidence of Marksville archaeology. In essence, the project consists of documenting as closely as possible the archaeological work carried out at Marksville to date, and analyzing the site collections that resulted. As such, it is an exercise in analytic archaeology as defined by Rouse (1973:23-25) and uses artifacts—in this case exclusively ceramic—as the basic units of study. The approach is admittedly inductive and particularistic. No apology is offered for the emphasis on description and classification, however, for I consider both operations essential to the success of future research leading to higher levels of integration. As restated by Redman (1973:19),

> the classification of artifacts affects all later work and provides the perspective through which past behavior is investigated.

In the case of Marksville, it is necessary to start at the beginning and rebuild a valid perspective capable of supporting the synthetic and comparative archaeology defined by Rouse (1973).

The particularistic orientation, and sometimes overwhelming concern with ceramic minutiae, displayed herein should not imply that I do not espouse some of the more nomothetic goals of the "new archaeology." Nor is it likely that anyone could be more concerned with the subsistence, settlement pattern, or any other facet of the Marksville cultural system than I am. However, such problems can be faced only by archaeology that is still in the ground, and before initiating such new activity it would seem prudent to take stock of what can be learned from past archaeology at Marksville. Further, I believe there is a logical order in which investigations should proceed if there is to be any accuracy in the ultimate products we deliver. My views, then, would seem to coincide with the "senior archeologists" who "almost to a man . . . argue that 'processual archeology' cannot be carried out until *after* inductive archeology and culture history have been done . . ." (Flannery, 1973:49).

The following pages thus are viewed as a small, but necessary, first step towards an understanding of the Marksville cultural system. They describe the history of Marksville archaeology and ceramic collections from the site. The description is reinforced by typology and stratigraphy in an effort to isolate specific ceramic variables that can be used to date the site features and eventually to fit the Marksville site into a framework of archaeological phases that covers the entire Lower Mississippi Valley.[1] Tight control of the time and space variables through ceramics will hopefully provide the synchronic perspective necessary to build an accurate model of the interaction among Marksville sites and between Marksville sites and more distant areas including the northern Hopewell centers.

[1] An historical integration of the Marksville period in the Lower Mississippi Valley has already been published (Phillips, 1970:886-901). A large body of new data is currently being employed to update and expand this distribution of site components and phases, but the basic outline of Phillips' reconstruction remains a valid and extremely useful integrative framework.

I

A BACKGROUND FOR MARKSVILLE ARCHAEOLOGY

THE Marksville site in Avoyelles Parish, Louisiana is well known to American archaeologists as the classic example of a Hopewellian expression in the southeastern United States. The site lends its name to most of the Hopewellian pottery types in the Lower Mississippi Valley as well as to the classic Hopewellian phase of the area. Indeed, the name Marksville has virtually displaced the name Hopewell when talking about Middle Woodland sites and cultures in the Lower Valley and adjacent areas. It is, therefore, most unfortunate that so dominating a site as Marksville has remained in many important respects the "mystery site."

Marksville may be a mystery site to most students of American prehistory, but this is not because of any lack of archaeology at the site. Vast quantities of earth have been moved to expose the story of its occupation. In fact, so much earth has been moved that Winslow Walker, after visiting the site in July of 1931, was moved to write:

> The Marksville group has been worked over by several investigators, the result being that such mounds as have escaped levelling under the process of cultivation present the appearance of small craters, good sized pits having been scooped out of the tops, or else they are merely shells of mounds left after the digging of broad trenches through their centers. (Walker, 1932:172)

Two major excavations at Marksville were carried out after Walker's visit! Marksville must be one of the most thoroughly explored sites in the Lower Mississippi Valley. Why, then, the mystery?

As other cultural periods were broken down into tightly defined phases, the Marksville period was left largely in limbo, awaiting long delayed site reports. Few people had seen or handled the pottery from Marksville. The Crooks site report (Ford and Willey, 1940) remained the only description of Marksville culture. As survey work progressed in the Yazoo and Tensas basins, few sites were located that produced crosshatched rims and the other diagnostic Marksville ceramic traits. The result was that only the latest part of the Marksville sequence, the Issaquena phase, received adequate description (Greengo, 1964; Phillips, 1970). The much needed description of the classic Marksville phase must come from material collected on the Marksville Prairie.

The aim of this chapter is to concentrate in one place as much data as can be corralled on Marksville archaeology. It is not meant to be, and it cannot be, a substitute for the needed site reports. They may never happen. The sad reality of the situation is that so much time has elapsed between the actual field work and the present that much of the necessary information has been lost—especially that most perishable form of data that is stored solely in the minds of men. Collections, field notes, photographs, and other records have been scattered across the country to a number of museums and other institutions. Conflicts that arise in attempting to collate the records of Marksville archaeology are many, and some may never be resolved. Despite these problems and frustrations, a great deal of sound information on Marksville is available. It is presented here to aid in understanding Marksville archaeology and as a base for future research.

THE SETTING

To say that the geographical location of the Marksville site determined the vigorous cultural development that took place there would be an unjustifiable case of reductionism. However, the strategic location of the site must be considered a factor of importance in any attempt to understand the process through which cultural forces from several directions merged to form that distinct entity known as Marksville culture. Situated atop a relic alluvial plain of Pleistocene age and surrounded by rich bottomlands, Marksville is an ideal location from which to exploit several different environments. Perhaps more important from the standpoint of overall cultural development, Marksville is located near the junction of two major river valleys. The valleys of both the Mississippi and Red rivers were ideal avenues for the spread of ideas and raw materials. An inspection of local geography and geology is a necessary beginning, then, for an understanding of Marksville culture.

Marksville geography

The Marksville site is located about a mile east of a town with the same name in Avoyelles Parish, Louisiana (Fig. 1). The area enjoys a mild temperate climate with abundant rainfall, averaging 56.7 inches annually. Thermometer

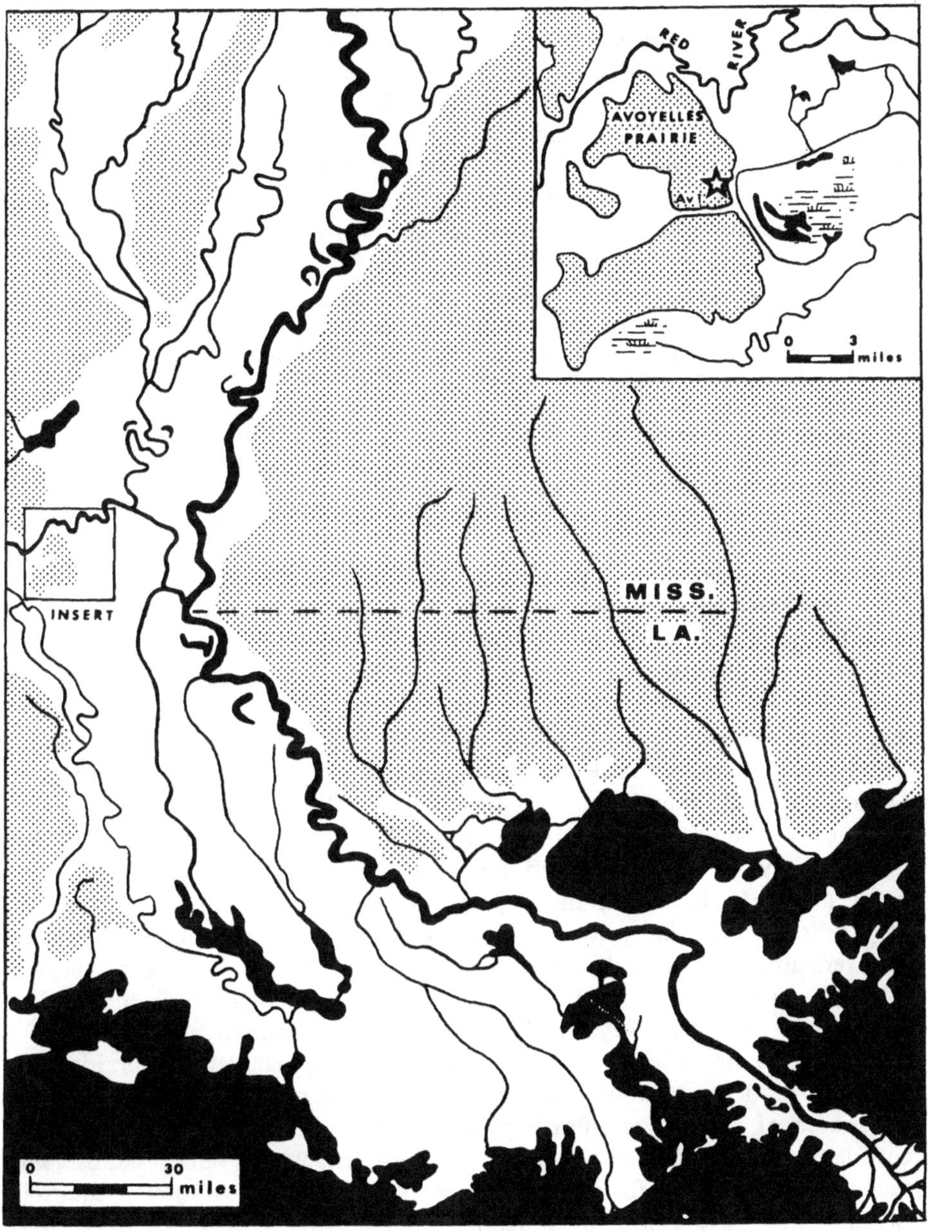

Fig. 1. Marksville site location

readings rarely fall below 20 degrees Fahrenheit in winter and average highs are between 70 and 100 degrees during the remainder of the year.

The most outstanding topographic feature at the Marksville site is the sharp dichotomy between prairie and floodplain. Marksville sits on the eastern edge of the Marksville Prairie overlooking Old River and adjacent bottomlands some thirty-five to forty feet below. In a style of writing seldom duplicated in the twentieth century, Skipwith (1881:110) captures the impression that strangers must have had as they approached the site during its ascendancy:

> Penetrating the parish from Simmsport to Moreauville, the entire route upon nearly the same level, a stranger who emerges from the swamp and sees for the first time the Marksville prairie towering fifty feet above him, presenting to his astonished vision the appearance of frowning battlements of some venerable fortress, at first view it seems as though an impassable barrier to his further progress has been conjured up by some wonderful upheaval of nature; but as he draws nearer and scans the marks of unquestionable antiquity and winds his devious way until he finds a road almost as steep as the Tarpeian rock, awe and wonderment give place to curiosity.

During those times of the year when flood conditions prevail in the alluvial valley, the Marksville Prairie is an especially favorable location.

The prairie environment at Marksville is described in a journal entry of William Dunbar written in 1804 as "... very level, only a few clumps of trees to be seen, all covered with good grass" (O'Pry, 1928:32). The small streams which drain the prairie are bordered by a narrow fringe of trees which include water oak, cherrybark oak, post oak, green ash, American elm, redgum, hickory, cow oak, hawthorns, and loblolly pine (Brown, 1944, 1945). Similar vegetation is found along the rim of the well-drained escarpment. The prairie is marked by depressions which are more poorly drained than the prairie proper (Fisk, 1940:76). In the depressions, depending upon the amount of water present, may be growths of red maple, green ash, water oak, winged elm, redgum, willow oak, swamp blackgum, and bald cypress (Brown, 1945:10). Freeman and Custis (1806) add the candleberry bush, holly, dogwood, sassafras, and buckeye to the list of prairie vegetation.

A moderate amount of animal life probably shared the prairie with Marksville residents, although the nearby floodplain was likely more important as a source of game. The animal species inhabiting the prairie during the first centuries of the Christian Era were no doubt much the same as those wild species that can be found around Marksville today. Rabbits, squirrels, opossum, deer, a plethora of songbirds, and a wide variety of snakes were possibly of most interest to the aboriginal population.

A second environment, the floodplain, is even richer in natural resources and separated from the Marksville site only by Old River and a difference of roughly forty feet in elevation. The floodplain environment is marked by those landforms normally characteristic of meander belts. Alluviation has had a leveling effect so that the primary topographic features consist of low parallel ridges and swales. The ridges represent natural levees formed by meandering streams and consist predominantly of well-drained silty and sandy clays. The swales drain poorly and are filled with thick deposits of clays and silts. They support a dense swamp or forest vegetation. Abandoned channels are conspicuous floodplain features and vary in degrees of filling from nearly open oxbow lakes to completely filled "clay plugs" (Saucier, 1971:27). Most of the floodplain to the east of Marksville is subject to seasonal backwater overflow.

Mixed bottomland hardwoods make up the primary forest type in the floodplain (Hayes, 1945:30). Drainage is extremely important in determining specific forest growth in such an environment, and a difference of only a few inches in elevation can produce different tree covers (Brown, 1945:8). The wettest areas normally contain bald cypress, swamp red maple, tupelo gum, Drummond red maple, water ash, and pumpkin ash. Poorly drained soils toward the bases of natural levees are covered with growths of overcup oak, willow, bitter pecan, green ash, water oak, and hawthorn. Redgum, cottonwood, American sycamore, black willow, locust, and hackberry can be found along the margins of sandy streams and in all areas of deposited silt. Natural levees, the highest ground in the foodplain, are topped with redgum, cherrybark oak, willow oak, cow oak, Nuttal oak, American elm, winged elm, and persimmon.

Long after being abandoned as a channel of the Mississippi, Old River flowed slowly north past the Marksville site to empty eventually, through Little River and a complex system of bayous, into the Red River. The network of bayous and rivers provided not only drainage for the bottomlands, but also a convenient means of transportation by which to exploit the floodplain environment. The many miles of waterways penetrated the remotest regions of the swamps and ultimately connected with both the Mississippi and Red rivers for continued travel to even more distant locations. Old River remained an important avenue of transportation as late as the steamboat era (Saucier, 1943:173). It was finally dammed opposite the northern end of the Marksville site in 1933.

Very little is known as yet about the diet of Marksville's inhabitants, but it is not unreasonable to speculate that the floodplain must have been attractive to them as a source of animal life. Even today, an incredible abundance of game of all sorts is there for the taking. Fish are plentiful and almost surely were an important source of animal protein. The area is on the Mississippi Flyway, and the maze of lakes and streams is still one of the major wintering grounds for numerous species of waterfowl. The floodplain environment offered a wide assortment of mammals as well; white-tail deer, black bear, opossum, raccoon, bobcat, red squirrel, grey fox, and swamp rabbit are only a partial sample of the wide selection of game reserves that might have been exploited. In short, it can be predicted that the nearby floodplain provided a food supply fully capable of sustaining a substantial Marksville population on the prairie above, even without the supplement of agriculture.

Marksville geology

Compared with most land surfaces in the Lower Mississippi Valley, the ground on which the Marksville site is located is ancient. The prairie terrace at Marksville consists of relic alluvial plains of the Red and Mississippi rivers which were formed during the Sangamon Interglacial Stage between 80,000 and 100,000 years ago (Saucier, 1971:44). Geologically, the period was one of slow valley aggradation in which glacial outwash deposits of sands and gravels were dropped initially, followed by deposition of fine-grained sediments through meander belt and backswamp formation. The prairie terrace around Marksville is characterized by a distinctive meander belt with numerous abandoned channels (Ibid.:17).

The Marksville Prairie represents a segment of the western escarpment of the Mississippi alluvial valley (Fisk, 1940:25); the bluffs adjacent to the Marksville site were cut by the Mississippi River when it occupied its westernmost course since the last glaciation. After following a western course for some time, the Mississippi gradually moved to the east, finally ending up in its present meander belt. The easterly movement of the Mississippi is responsible for much of the floodplain topography in the bottomlands east of Marksville. Numerous parallel ridges and swales mark the easterly migration of the Mississippi away from its course at the edge of the Marksville Prairie. The Red River entered some of the abandoned Mississippi channels and followed them to the new course of the master stream (Fisk, 1940:45).

Interpretations of the geology of the Lower Mississippi Valley have a direct bearing on Marksville archaeology. For a complete understanding of the settlement at Marksville, including detailed knowledge of the environment and relationships to major trade networks, it is imperative to know the position of the Mississippi River during the centuries of site occupation. As opinions on the chronology of the Mississippi River's meander belts have changed, so have speculations on the relationship of the Marksville site to the Mississippi River. Such parallel development is not surprising since research efforts in the geology and in the archaeology of the Lower Mississippi Valley have been closely allied.

Most investigators have assumed that the channel now occupied by Old River was an open stream at the time the Marksville site was occupied. In an early study of the geology of the Lower Red River area, Chawner (1936) postulated a Tensas-Black channel of the Mississippi that went through Lake

Long, through Bayou Avoyelles, past the Marksville site via Old River, and on into Bayou des Glaises. Chawner (1936:45) estimated that the Tensas-Black Channel was abandoned less than 1,000 years ago. His estimate was based on the compressed archaeological chronology of the time and assumed that Marksville was situated adjacent to the Mississippi River during its occupation.

Fisk (1940:28) disagreed with Chawner's assertion that part of the Tensas-Black channel would have used Old River as a connector. Instead, he postulated an earlier course past the site that followed Bayou Cocodrie, Larto Lake, Little River, and Old River. In a later study, Fisk (1944:42) included Old River as a segment of the Mississippi's stage 3 channel which he estimated as dating to 300 A.D. Both Ford (1951) and Vescelius (1957) accepted Fisk's stage 3 association and assumed that the Marksville site was occupied at 300 A.D. or later.

The most recent assessment of Lower Valley chronology (Saucier, 1971) suggests a considerably revised geologic history for the floodplain adjacent to the Marksville site. Saucier's proposed meander belt 3, called the Cocodrie meander belt south of Natchez and the Sunflower meander belt to the north, is the one which passes the Marksville site (Saucier, 1971:57). Meander belt 3 is traced directly into Teche Ridge along the western side of the alluvial valley and downstream into the Teche Subdelta. The estimated date of meander belt 3 is from 6000 to 4500 years before present, or roughly 4000 to 2500 B.C. (Saucier, 1971:45). The beginning date for meander belt 3 marks the change of the last segment of the Mississippi from braided to meandering. Saucier (1971:62) believes that after meander belt 3 was abandoned, the Mississippi River moved gradually east to its present meander belt, number 5, which began about 2800 years ago.

Saucier's new chronology would mean that the Mississippi River was well to the east of the Marksville site during the centuries of occupation. In fact, if Saucier is correct, the Mississippi attained its present meander belt by 800 B.C. Thus, earlier speculations that the inhabitants of Marksville occupied a site atop a bluff overlooking the Mississippi River are no longer justified. Instead, it appears that long after the bluff was carved a population settled at Marksville and constructed the extensive earthworks and mounds. At that time, an ancient channel of the Mississippi was occupied by Old River which was probably an open stream draining the floodplain and eventually connecting with the Red and Mississippi rivers through a complex system of lakes and bayous.

Site features

The main part of the Marksville site is enclosed by a semicircular embankment about 3,300 feet long which ranges from three to seven feet in

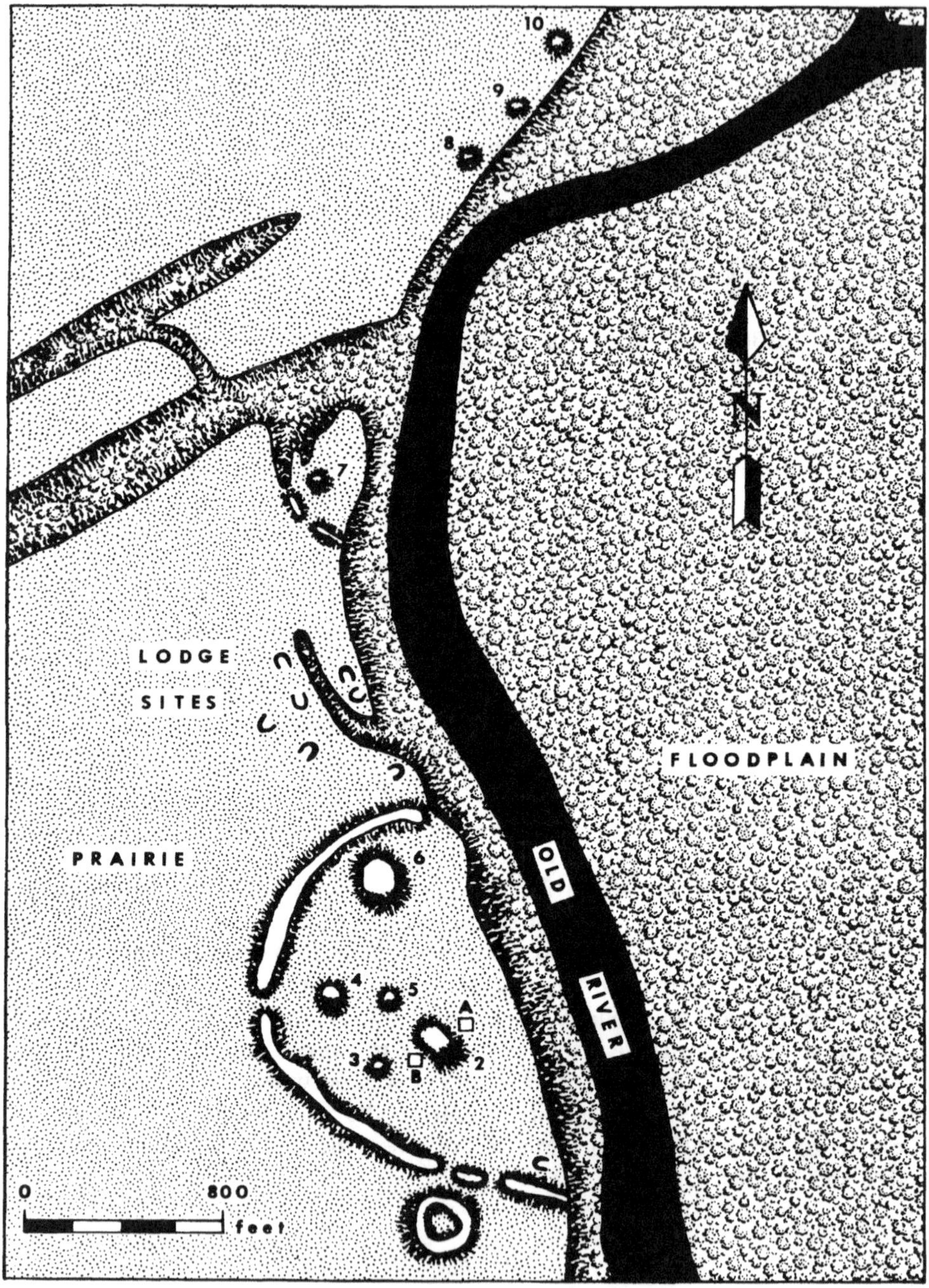

Fig. 2. The Marksville site

height (Fowke, 1928:412). The open end of the enclosure borders the edge of a bluff which descends to Old River (Fig. 2). The purpose of the enclosure appears to be ceremonial rather than protective as there is an opening on the western side of the embankment and two more on the southern end. It is likely that the earthworks were built to delineate a special area in which the dead were buried and other formal affairs were handled. Midden areas within the enclosure indicate that at some point it was used as a village area as well.

Five mounds of varying sizes and shapes are located within the main enclosure. By convention, these mounds and others in the Marksville locality are designated by the numbers given them on Fowke's original site map (Fowke, 1928:plate 64). The northernmost, Mound 6, is a truncated structure about 300 feet in diameter and thirteen feet in height (Ibid.: 422). Toward the center of the enclosure are two conical mounds: Mound 4 is 100 feet in diameter and twenty feet high; Mound 5 is seventy feet in diameter and only three and a half feet high (Ibid.: 414,422). In the southern half of the enclosure is Mound 2 which may have been a flat-topped structure of rectangular shape. It is roughly 290 feet by 235 feet in lateral dimensions and fourteen feet high (Vescelius, 1957:417). Finally, there is Mound 3 which is another small conical mound sixty feet in diameter and three and a half feet high.

Several hundred feet to the south of the main enclosure is a smaller one. It is fairly circular, except for a flat side facing the main enclosure, and is about 300 feet in diameter (Fowke, 1928:413). The embankment forming the circle is twenty feet wide and two feet high.

A final embankment, about one third of a mile to the north of the main earthworks, takes advantage of the natural landscape to form another enclosure. The embankment is about 500 feet long and constructed so as to mark off a section of the Marksville Prairie that projects out from the main line of bluffs. Adjacent to the embankment, which is three to five feet in height, is a "moat" or borrow area several feet in depth. Thus, on the southwestern edge of the earthworks the distance from the top of the embankment to the bottom of the ditch is nearly ten feet (Fowke, 1928:412). The northern enclosure contains one pyramidal mound, number 7, about 100 feet square and six feet high. Fowke (1928:423) describes it as a smaller version of Mound 6.

There are a number of additional mounds scattered along the edge of the Marksville Prairie to the north of the three enclosures. Of these, only Mound 8 can be assigned securely to the Marksville period. It is a conical mound approximately fifteen feet high and eighty feet in diameter (Fowke, 1928:423). The possibility that some of the other mounds, such as mounds 9, 10, and 12, are of Marksville origin cannot be ruled out at the present time.

The main features of the Marksville site proper, the central enclosure and its mounds, can be seen clearly in Figures 3 and 4 which are aerial

Fig. 3. Aerial view of the Marksville site in the 1930's. Photograph by Col. Dache Reeves, USAF. The orientation is north.

Fig. 4. Aerial view of the Marksville site in the 1930's. Photograph by Col. Dache Reeves, USAF. The orientation is southeast.

photographs taken in the 1930s by the late Dache Reeves, then a U.S. Army major. The negatives of these and other aerial photographs of the site are on file in the U.S. National Museum. The photographs show numerous circular features outside the main earthworks, many of which correspond to the "lodge sites" shown by Fowke (1928:plate 64) on his site map. The majority of these features have been destroyed permanently in recent years by a housing subdivision, but a few remain intact and need immediate testing if there true function is to be discovered. The most obvious explanation for the circular features is the hypothesis that they represent the adjacent dwelling sites of the population that constructed the Marksville earthworks. However, at least two of these features have been tested without positive results. It is not impossible, therefore, that some of the circular scars could be the result of natural processes.

HISTORY OF MARKSVILLE ARCHAEOLOGY

The Marksville site has withstood a substantial amount of digging activity, but unfortunately most of the information on the artifacts recovered remains a mystery to everyone except those present at the excavations. Fowke's reports (1927, 1928) reveal that local antiquarians were aware that the mounds were not empty. He claims, for example, that the central part of Mound 8 had been trenched previously and that Mound 9 had been virtually destroyed by treasure seekers. It is doubtful that anything will ever be known about the artifacts recovered by the early pothunters.

Realistically, the story of Marksville archaeology revolves around three major expeditions: that of Gerard Fowke in 1926; that of Frank M. Setzler and James A. Ford in 1933; and that of Robert S. Neitzel and Edwin B. Doran in 1939. Most of the artifacts from Marksville that are available for study were recovered by one or another of these excavations. A rather tedious review of the nature and scope of previous Marksville archaeology is presented both for its historical interest and for background provenience information on the ceramics that will be described in the next chapter.

Early references

Marksville is one of the few Middle Woodland sites in the Southeast with earthworks rivaling those of the Ohio Valley; it is surprising to find very few early references which note its existence. One of the oldest published descriptions of the site can be found in the New Orleans *Daily Picayune* of 1 August 1851. Under the headline "HERNANDO DESOTO," the following article from the Marksville *Prairie Star* is reprinted:

> Since we have been in this place we have made a visit to old river, situated about one mile back of Marksville. Much had been said about the curious and apparently military works, the sign of which seems designed to remain as long as the world stands. We will first attempt a description, before we presume an opinion.
>
> The banks of what doubtless was once Red River, is about seventeen feet higher than the highest water marks ever known by the oldest inhabitants. Immediately upon the bank is situated a large mound, about twenty feet high, forming a level of about an acre on top; from this, or rather from the base of it, commences apparently a breastwork, of one mile in extent, forming a complete semicircle, uniformly eight feet in height, with a complete circumvalation the whole extent, with a slight interruption, however, of what appears to have been planted a battery for the use of the cannon.
>
> Immediately in the rear of this battery is situated a small mound, forty feet high, as though it was intended as a kind of look-out. Back of this, still, is another, built in the form of the Pyramyd of Cholula, a double mound, one upon the other, diminishing in size to the top. Some years since the Hon. P. Soulé and Judge Preston visited these ruins, and the opinion of the former was that they presented the appearance of European works. If we bear in mind the fact that this is the first high lands, not subject to overflow, after leaving the mouth of Red River, we are irresistibly led to the conclusion that it formed the camping ground of Hernando DeSoto; still the timber in some places appears to be quite ancient, some measuring six feet in diameter.

Since the unidentified reporter recorded his observations at a time when the Marksville site must have been relatively undisturbed by modern forces, the account is an important source of information on the original size and shape of the mounds. The mound heights, however, should be used cautiously as they deviate considerably from the dimensions computed by Fowke in 1926. A height of eight feet for the semicircular embankment is very plausible. As to identifications, there can be little doubt that the large, flat-topped mound is Mound 6, the "look-out" is Mound 4, and the "double mound" is Mound 2. The magnitude of Mississippi Valley flooding prior to the recent construction of artificial levees is admirably documented by the note on high water marks.

One salient feature of the 1851 description of the site at Marksville is that its construction is attributed, not to an aboriginal population, but to De Soto and his army. A similar perspective can be seen in another early reference to the site which is included in a description by Skipwith (1881:110) of the Marksville Prairie:

> Along the eastern margin of this prairie the Red River once flowed, and upon its northeastern margin, almost within the corporate limits of Marksville, are still to be seen the well-defined lineaments of an earthwork, crescent in form, too laboriously constructed and too skillfully laid off to warrant the opinion that it was the work of any savage tribe.

Although Skipwith clearly is talking about the Marksville site, his description is rather lacking in detail. No attempt is made to identify the builders of the earthworks except to surmise that the degree of sophistication exhibited is beyond the nineteenth century conception of aboriginal capabilities.

Realization that the Marksville site might be related to other mound sites being studied throughout the eastern United States was brought to professional attention in 1883 through correspondence from George Williamson to the Smithsonian Institution. The Williamson correspondence is summarized as follows:

> WILLIAMSON, GEORGE, calls attention to works near Marksville, La. South of that place is an embankment extending from a bluff on an old channel of the Red or some other river, a distance of a mile or more. The embankment is from 8 to 12 feet high and is flanked on the outside by a wide, deep ditch. In several places appear to have been sally-ports, and large old forest trees are growing on the bank. Inside the work are two large mounds, one of them covering several acres. In this vicinity are a great many mounds, some of them of great size. The remains are on the first high land on the bank of what was once a river channel, communicating with the Atchafalaya. (Williamson, 1883:686)

The estimate of eight to twelve feet for the height of the embankment supports the 1851 appraisal, and the mention of a ditch along the outside provides a new detail which is later confirmed by Fowke (1928:412 and plate 66a). Other aspects of Williamson's site description are poor in detail, but they conform in general to the earlier reports.

Perhaps the first description of the Marksville site to include mounds outside the main enclosure is found in a short article by George E. Beyer discussing the proceedings of the Louisiana Historical Society for 1899-1900. Beyer (1900:33) mentions that Prof. H. E. Chambers gave an account of a visit he made to Marksville during which he located "... a line of mounds, twelve in number, at intervals of about a mile extending due North and South." These must be the same twelve mounds that Fowke (1928: plate 64) shows along the eastern edge of the Marksville Prairie overlooking Old River. Beyer (1900:33) goes on to relate Chamber's description of the Marksville site:

> Prof. Chambers described an embankment that seemed to him of unusual character; bow shaped, about a mile long, and terminating in a series of small circular closely connected mounds; the line of earthworks quite symmetrical, rounded on the outer face and sloping to the inner; the whole covered by a dense forest growth. Local tradition attributes the work to De Soto and his men.

Details of site features within the main enclosure do not amplify those contained in the nineteenth century references. What is interesting is that as late as 1900 local tradition still credited De Soto with the construction of the Marksville site. Indeed, the folk tradition persisted even later, for while collecting Tunica myths at Marksville in the 1930s Mary Haas was told by Sesostrie Youchigant, the last fluent speaker of Tunica, that the Marksville mounds contained Spanish war dead:

> When the Spanish came here they were constantly fighting wars. Having picked up the dead and piled them all together, they would cover them up on the ground. The mounds which they placed on Red River go (along) near the bank. Where they fought, the mounds (which) they placed are still seen. (Haas, 1950:143)

With the tenacious De Soto legend going back at least as far as 1851 and continuing, even among the Indian population, as late as the time of the major twentieth century excavations, it is perhaps not so surprising after all that there are so few early references to the Marksville site.

Finally, one of the earliest published photographs of the Marksville site appears in Swanton's compendium on Indian tribes of the Lower Mississippi Valley (Swanton, 1911: plate 12). The photograph shows Mound 6 as viewed to the northeast across the village area from Mound 4. The caption underneath the photograph confirms the provenience identification and acknowledges that "...one or two other low, flat mounds lie toward the east near the banks of Old River."

Excavation by Fowke

The first scientific exploration of the Marksville site was that of Fowke in the spring of 1926. One of the most productive results of Fowke's three months of field work at Marksville was a detailed map of the site. His map (Fig. 5), which includes the Nick and Greenhouse sites as well as Marksville, has been used repeatedly in virtually all subsequent reports and illustrations of the site. Although recent aerial photographs suggest that Fowke's map has some distortion of scale from north to south, the detail within the main enclosure of the site is accurate and has been adopted herein. Fowke's major report (1928) supplements his map with complete descriptions of the external configurations of all the mounds and other site features.

In addition to mapping the site, Fowke excavated parts of two burial mounds which can be assigned with confidence to the classic Marksville phase of site occupation. The mounds are numbers 4 and 8. Mound 4 is located within enclosure A and Mound 8 sits on the edge of the bluff just under a mile to the north. Fowke also explored three other conical mounds in the

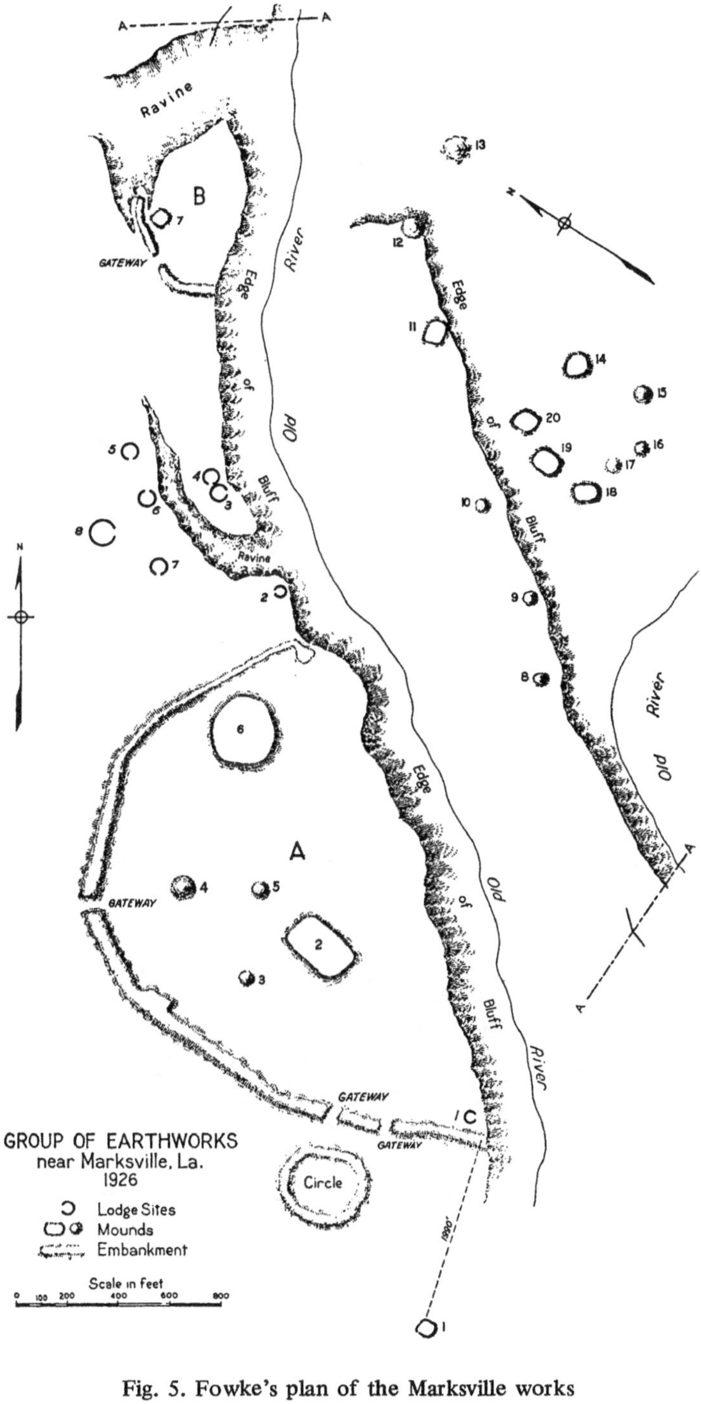

Fig. 5. Fowke's plan of the Marksville works

vicinity of the site, Mounds 3, 10, and 12, but these cannot be assigned safely to the Marksville period. In fact, there is no evidence that these were even burial mounds.

Mound 4.–Having identified Mound 4 as the largest conical mound at the site, Fowke selected it for excavation with expectations that it would be equal in yield to remains of the "Mound Builders" in other parts of the country. In classic form, he went straight for the center, hoping all the while to find a rich central grave below the mound. Fowke's trench was twenty-five feet wide and sixty feet in length (Fowke, 1928:415). It began at the south edge of Mound 4 and extended ten feet past the center. The trench reached into sterile soil below the mound over its entire length. A view of Fowke's trench as it was found by Setzler in 1933 can be seen in Figure 6. Another photograph of the trench during actual excavation was published by Fowke (1928: plate 67*a*).

Fowke found burials in seventeen locations within his trench (Fowke, 1928:421), but he did not find a central grave below the mound. Instead, he discovered that the mound began with a clay platform on which a number of burials were placed (Ibid.: 420). Postholes were noted on the platform (Ibid.: 421) suggesting that once it may have been the foundation for a building,

Fig. 6. Marksville Mound 4 showing remains of Fowke's trench. Photograph by Setzler in 1933.

perhaps one in which the dead were stored until enough remains had accumulated to erect a mound. The burial platform was covered with a mantle of mottled clay which contained a few scattered burials (Ibid.: 422). Later, two pits containing a number of additional burials were dug into the top of the primary mound and a second clay mantle was added to complete the mound. Fowke's report (1928) thus outlines the basic stratigraphy of Mound 4. He did not enlarge his trench any farther, apparently because of excessive rains and what he thought to be disappointing results.

Mound 8.–The other Marksville period mound which Fowke explored, Mound 8, had been trenched previously but the earlier excavations did not reach to the base (Ibid.: 423). Fowke began a new trench, fifteen feet wide, from the southeast edge of the mound. The trench extended to three feet past the center of the mound by which time it had widened to twenty feet (Ibid.: 423). The entire mound consisted of mixed pockets of grey and sandy yellow clays which were of the same character as the subsoil. A view of the remains of Mound 8 as found by Setzler in 1933 is provided in Figure 7. Fowke (1928: plate 67*b*) also illustrates Mound 8 during the actual excavations.

By his efforts, Fowke located seven graves in Mound 8 which contained badly decayed bones and a total of four vessels. The graves were covered with

Fig. 7. Remains of Marksville Mound 8 after excavation by Fowke. Photograph by Setzler in 1933.

cane matting and all were sunk into the subsoil (Ibid.: 424). Nowhere in his report does Fowke mention any trace of a burial platform in Mound 8. The clays composing the mound rested on the natural surface (Ibid.: 423) and all the burials were in graves dug into the subsoil. No burials are mentioned as being found in the mound fill. In short, Fowke's description of Mound 8 suggests a considerably different burial situation than that found in Mound 4.

Mounds 3, 10, and 12.—The three other conical mounds that Fowke tested must be mentioned in passing since the possibility cannot be ruled out that they might date from the Marksville period. Mound 3 was within the main enclosure and greatly reduced through cultivation by the time Fowke saw it. The circular cut, twenty feet in diameter, which he dug into the center of Mound 3 extended down into sterile soil. Fowke found absolutely nothing in the mound except a small hearth on the natural surface beneath it (Fowke, 1928:414).

Fowke's method in Mound 10 also consisted of digging a circular cut, twenty feet in diameter, through the center of the mound into sterile soil. This time he found potsherds, bits of charcoal, and some chert (Ibid.: 425), but again no sign of burials or mound stratigraphy. The ceramic material he found, if saved at all, has never been reported and is not available for analysis. Fowke did find several other artifacts in Mound 10 that merit comment. He found "two small pieces of grooved burned clay similar to those occurring so abundantly north of Delhi" (Ibid.: 425). These certainly must be examples of one of the grooved varieties of Poverty Point objects, something that does not turn up in the other collections from Marksville.[2] He also found a highly polished plummet of "magnetic iron ore" (Ibid.: 425) which gives any additional indication that Mound 10 may represent a pre-Marksville component in the vicinity of the site. Some of the material from Mound 10 is illustrated by Setzler (1933*b*: plate 6).

Finally, Mound 12 was a more complicated structure which was apparently built in three stages. Fowke began with a circular cut in the middle of the mound but this became too deep for removal of backdirt so a trench, fourteen feet wide, was added from the south (Fowke, 1928:426-27). The mound contained two used floors, potsherds, animal bone, and chert but no trace of human burials. Again, the ceramic material is unavailable for study and the cultural affiliation of Mound 12 cannot be determined at this time.[3]

Reports.—Details of Fowke's excavations at Marksville are provided in his preliminary report (Fowke, 1927) and in his final report (Fowke, 1928).

[2] A recent search at the U.S. National Museum, Smithsonian Institution, failed to locate any ceramic material from Mound 10. The two fired clay objects, however, were examined and confirmed to be examples of the cylindrical grooved variety of Poverty Point objects as defined by Ford and Webb (1956:41).

[3] Ceramic material from Mound 12 was not present in the Marksville collections at the U.S. National Museum.

While these reports offer a full account of the extent of Fowke's work and the structure of each mound he opened, they have little in the way of illustrations or detailed descriptions of the material he recovered. The preliminary report (Fowke, 1927: Figs. 246-47) illustrates only three vessels and the final report is totally devoid of artifact illustrations.

Swanton's contribution

The trench which Fowke cut into Mound 4 was never closed, and in 1930 it yielded additional ceramic material. John R. Swanton visited Marksville in July of that year while making an ethnological reconnaissance of Louisiana (Setzler, 1933*b*:1). Swanton managed to extract portions of two decorated vessels and a number of potsherds from Fowke's unfinished trench.[4] The material acquired by Swanton joined that of Fowke in the U.S. National Museum.

Setzler's recognition of Hopewellian connections

Since Fowke's reports contained so few artifact illustrations, it is fortunate that Frank M. Setzler recognized the great similarity between the vessels Fowke found at Marksville and those characteristic of northern Hopewell. As early as 1933 Setzler stressed connections with the Ohio Valley which was the best known Hopewellian center at the time (Setzler, 1933*a*: 153). In the same year he published a complete description of the pottery that Fowke recovered in Mounds 4 and 8 (Setzler, 1933*b*). The report included excellent photographs of some of the finest examples of Marksville pottery. While strongly stressing the ceramic similarities between Marksville and Ohio Hopewell, Setzler recognized that the internal structures of mounds 4 and 8 were not "typical" of northern Hopewell and that the Marksville burials lacked a great many other kinds of diagnostic Hopewellian artifacts (Setzler, 1933*b*:7-8). In later writings, perhaps as a result of Ford's influence, Setzler went on to postulate that Marksville was the cultural base which inspired the development of northern Hopewell (Setzler & Strong, 1936:306; Setzler, 1940:262-66).

Excavation by Setzler and Ford

Since Marksville was the first site in the Lower Mississippi Valley and, indeed, one of the first sites in the entire Southeast to demonstrate close

[4] The decorated vessels include a small beaker, 7.6 cm in height and 9.2 cm in maximum diameter, and a tubby pot 13.0 cm in height and 13.1 cm in maximum diameter. Both vessels are classified as Marksville Stamped, *var. Marksville*.

affinity to northern Hopewell, it is not surprising that after Setzler's recognition the site was immediately the scene of intense excavations. The main part of the site, Enclosure A, was acquired by the town of Marksville in June 1933 for development as a park (Setzler, 1934:38). That August, Setzler arrived with his assistant, James A. Ford, to continue investigations and supervise restorations. Their work extended from August 22 to December 1, 1933.

The main energies of Setzler and Ford were expended on further examination of Mound 4. After uncovering a substantial amount of additional information on this mound, they tested Mounds 5 and 6, a village area east of Mound 2, and "Site X" which was another village area to the east of Mound 6.

Reports.—Setzler (1934) mentions the 1933 Marksville excavations briefly, and Ford (1936:227-30) gives a short introductory account of the main ceramic types encountered. However, a detailed report of the work at Marksville by Setzler and Ford was never published. Apparently, the report was started since a manuscript entitled "Marksville: A Louisiana Variant of the Hopewell Culture" is alluded to many times as Setzler (n.d.) or Setzler (1939). In any case, the manuscript could not be located for incorporation into this study nor could any of the original field notes, profiles, or floor plans. A set of ninety-five negatives with annotations by Setzler on the negative jackets is the only supplementary material that could be found to provide a more complete record of the 1933 excavations.

Mound 4.—Photographs of Mound 4, taken by Setzler during the excavations, show that the mound was removed in five-foot cuts running east to west, or perpendicular to Fowke's trench. This slicing operation was carried on simultaneously from both the north and south sides of the mound. Figure 8 shows an early cross section on the south end of the mound. The area outlined to the right represents Fowke's trench and the soil that had washed back into it; the portion to the left is the undisturbed mound. Figure 9 illustrates the method of excavating five-foot cuts as well as an early cross section on the north end of the mound. The demarcation of the mound and subsoil can be seen clearly in the lower center of the photograph.

As excavations in Mound 4 progressed, it became apparent that Fowke's trench had passed through one end of a large burial chamber which had been dug into the clay platform at the base of the mound. In Ford's words,

> It was determined that some of the burials recovered by Fowke had been enclosed in a large square burial vault of earth which was covered by layers of canes and clay. This central chamber occupied the larger part of the mound. (Ford, 1936:227)

The platform can be seen in Figure 10 which shows the south and west sides

Fig. 8. Early cross section of south trench, Marksville Mound 4, showing remains of Fowke's excavations. Photograph by Setzler in 1933.

Fig. 9. Early cross section of north trench, Marksville Mound 4, showing method of slicing by five-foot cuts. Photograph by Setzler in 1933.

Fig. 10. Burial platform at base of Marksville Mound 4 with timber imprints exposed along north side. Photograph by Setzler in 1933.

Fig. 11. Cross section of burial platform at base of Marksville Mound 4. Photograph by Setzler in 1933.

as well as the partially excavated burial chamber in the center. The stakes in this photograph are at five-foot intervals, suggesting that the platform was approximately twenty-five feet on a side. Figure 11 shows a cross section of the platform. The bottom line divides the platform from subsoil, and the upper line marks the top of the platform at five feet. Soil above the line at five feet is mixed with white, water-deposited soil from the platform surface which indicates that it was removed from the burial vault to the left.

The best description of the burial vault itself, as well as of the overall structure of Mound 4, is presumably a firsthand account written by Ford:

> A flat-topped structure about five feet high had been constructed and allowed to stand for some time. Then the center of the platform had been dug out and a square vault made which was covered with log rafters topped with layers of cane and clay. A number of burials were placed in the vault. Scattered burials were also made in small individual vaults on the surface of the platform. A primary mantle was then piled over the entire platform and its included vault. A few burials were scattered through the soil of the primary mantle. A secondary mantle was added later. (Ford and Willey, 1940:32)

The photographs taken by Setzler during the excavation confirm Ford's description but add little additional information. A row of imprints of the rafters forming the vault roof can be seen in Figure 12. The rafters were discovered under seven layers of bark and cane matting. They sloped in toward the burial chamber, thus demonstrating that the vault roof had collapsed from the weight of the mound. Figure 13 shows another view of the platform in which postholes of the vertical supports for the rafters are visible.

Whether or not Mound 4 was dismantled completely is known only by its excavators. Figure 14 records a stage in which very nearly all of the mound is gone. The tall pole in this photograph represents the center of the mound, and Setzler's annotation for this negative indicates that earth was piled to the top of the pole during restoration of the mound.

Traces of twelve burials were found in Mound 4 as well as a number of artifacts (Setzler, 1934:38). The catalog record in the U.S. National Museum reflects that Setzler and Ford uncovered seven decorated and six plain vessels in the mound in addition to great quantities of potsherds. Figure 15 shows Setzler working on one of the decorated vessels *in situ*. Provenience data within Mound 4 is not recorded for the potsherds, probably because it was not considered meaningful. Setzler (1934:38) says simply that "village debris, disclosed by numerous decorated potsherds, had largely been used as building material for the mound." Non-ceramic artifacts listed in the U.S. National Museum catalog include two platform pipes, fifteen projectile points, three stone knives, a quartz crystal, a copper fragment, and a piece of worked shell.

Mound 5.—Very little can be said about the excavation of Mound 5 which apparently was not very extensive. There are no pictures of the

Fig. 12. Imprints of rafters forming roof of burial vault in platform at base of Marksville Mound 4. Photograph by Setzler in 1933.

Fig. 13. Burial platform at base of Marksville Mound 4 with postholes marking vertical supports for vault roof. Photograph by Setzler in 1933.

Fig. 14. Excavations in Marksville Mound 4. Photograph by Setzler in 1933.

Fig. 15. Frank M. Setzler uncovering vessel in south trench, Marksville Mound 4. Photograph possibly by Ford in 1933.

excavation in Setzler's photographic record, which is so complete for Mound 4. A brief note in the Crooks report sums up the Mound 5 excavations in the following way: "Excavation in the small structure discovered no burials. Neither was it possible to determine its shape." (Ford & Willey, 1940:32). A small collection of potsherds in the U.S. National Museum confirms that Setzler and Ford did find some material in the mound. It is said to come from a trench, twenty feet wide, dug through the central part of the mound. The pottery is classic Marksville, thus demonstrating at the minimum that the mound was constructed of Marksville midden. Probably, Fowke's speculation (1928:422) that Mound 5 represents a burial platform or an unfinished burial mound is warranted. An unfinished mound or platform next to a completed large conical mound parallels the arrangement at Crooks.

Mound 6.—If little is known about excavations in Mound 5, the situation concerning Mound 6 is even more mysterious. There are absolutely no published descriptions, however superficial, on the work Setzler and Ford did in Mound 6. One would begin to wonder whether the largest mound at the site were touched at all were it not for a few photographs taken by Setzler and a simple declaration by Ford (1936:230) that "further excavations were made in the large truncate mound 6 . . ."

The excavations in Mound 6 fell short of revealing the shape and internal structure of the mound, the date of its construction, and its relationship to the other mounds in the vicinity of Marksville. These important considerations will never be known until further work is performed at the site. Determination of the true shape and date of Mound 6 should be one of the primary aims of future Marksville archaeology. In the meanwhile, anything said about the mound must be treated as pure speculation.

Certain basic aspects of the Mound 6 excavations can be pieced together by a study of Setzler's photographs combined with his cursory annotations. A view of the mound before excavation (Fig. 16) shows a pattern of stakes at five-foot intervals which Setzler calls "the twenty-foot trench." By counting stakes, one discovers that the overall dimensions of the trench are twenty feet by sixty feet. There is no perspective to show exactly where on the mound the trench is located, but it appears to be on a flat area which is presumably the top center of the mound.

Setzler's photographs do not record any stratigraphy that might have been encountered except for frequent mention of a "habitation level" that is said to be a "few feet" below the surface. Apparently, the habitation level was so designated because of the discovery of postholes at that depth. Figure 17 shows Ford with his hand in one of the postholes and suggests that the habitation level was approximately three feet from the surface. Such a depth is also confirmed by Figures 18 and 19 which show additional views of excavations on the habitation level of Mound 6.

Fig. 16. The "twenty-foot trench" staked out on Marksville Mound 6 prior to excavation. Stakes at five-foot intervals. Photograph by Setzler.

Fig. 17. James A. Ford troweling out posthole in "habitation level" of Marksville Mound 6. Photograph by Setzler in 1933.

Fig. 18. Excavation on "habitation level" of Marksville Mound 6. James A. Ford in center of workers. Photograph by Setzler in 1933.

Fig. 19. Excavation on "habitation level" of Marksville Mound 6. Photograph by Setzler in 1933.

Although photographs of the Mound 6 exploration demonstrate that the area excavated was fairly extensive horizontally, none of them reveal that the trench went any deeper than the level visible in Figures 18 and 19. No evidence can be found to indicate that Setzler and Ford actually cut completely through Mound 6 to expose a full cross section. Since the photographs show balks separating five by twenty foot sections of the trench, it can be surmised that it was never the intention to expose a full profile of the mound. While this method of excavation is fine for test pits to determine relatively shallow village stratigraphy, it is hardly designed to get to the base of a mound which is thirteen feet in height.

A very important detail pertaining to the structure of Mound 6 has thus far been overlooked. Neitzel (October 1973, personal communication) recalls seeing a cross section sketch of Mound 6 which showed a small conical mound beginning in the habitation level and rising above the flat-topped surface of the mound. The portion of the conical structure above the surface of Mound 6 was drawn in dashed lines as if conjectured, but the base was clearly shown to begin within the excavated level of the mound. Neitzel believes he saw the sketch in Setzler's field notebook, but it is also possible that it was drawn for him during a discussion with Ford. Whatever the case, it is important to incorporate into the record the possibility of internal evidence within Mound 6 of a conical mound that may have topped the large truncated platform. The configuration is precisely that which is illustrated for Mound 6 in Ford's final reconstruction of the site (Ford, 1969: chart 2, plan 6), although there is good reason to question the accuracy of this drawing. Neitzel also recalls that formerly there was a house with a brick chimney, belonging to an Adolph Frank, atop Mound 6. The house burned sometime prior to 1898.

Finally, a comment on the aptness of the term "habitation level" can be delayed no longer. Material from Mound 6, along with that from all the other excavation units, went directly into the U.S. National Museum. Examination of the collections and the catalog record shows that the total yield of Mound 6 was thirteen decorated potsherds, a projectile point, a scraper, and a large hammerstone. Postholes or not, a collection of that size from Mound 6 hardly can be considered indicative of habitation. The fill of a structure the size of Mound 6 is more than likely to contain a few stray potsherds and other artifacts. There are no records of hearths, animal bones, shell, trash pits, or any of the other things normally encountered in occupational levels. In short, existing evidence from the Mound 6 excavations adds precious little information on the date or purpose of the largest Indian monument in the Marksville park.

Village area.—According to Ford (1936:227) the area of the Marksville site that yielded the richest surface collections was located between Mound 2 and the bluffs to the east. Speculating that the surface distribution reflected the situation underground, Setzler and Ford determined to excavate a trench in this most promising area of village midden. It was a very natural area in which to search for site stratigraphy.

In reconstructing this segment of the saga of Marksville archaeology, the main problem is in determining the exact size and location of the trench. Vescelius (1957: Fig. 1), apparently having had access to appropriate data, did not hesitate to show the Setzler and Ford trench on his site map. He illustrates a trench twenty feet wide which begins at the flanks of Mound 2 and runs 180 feet due east. The only photograph by Setzler of the village excavations (Fig. 20) may confirm a trench of the size indicated by Vescelius. People are shown excavating on each end of the trench and there is a mound in the background. If the mound is Mound 2, the orientation of mound to trench is wrong. Another possibility is that the photograph, labeled only as "Excavations in the Village Site," may be of the trench through Site X (described below), the mound then being Mound 6.

Whatever the truth about the photograph shown as Figure 20, the catalog notes in the U.S. National Museum are not in accord with the trench shown by Vescelius. The catalog notes are quite specific in describing the provenience of the artifacts recovered. For example, one group of artifacts is said to come from "VILLAGE SITE: CUT D, BETWEEN STAKES 5, 6, 8 & 9; SECTION

Fig. 20. Excavations in the village area at the Marksville site. Photograph by Setzler in 1933.

1, FROM SURFACE TO BASE OF PLOW LINE." Would that the provenience of all the material from Marksville were recorded so exactly!

The problem which arises is that all of the village material can be accounted for as coming from just six cuts, A through F, which fall between a total of twelve stakes. Figure 21 presents a schematic diagram of the only possible arrangement of cuts and stakes that is in accord with the provenience data recorded in the catalog of the U.S. National Museum. Unless cuts A through F represent only the ones from which village material was saved, there is no indication that a trench the size of that shown by Vescelius was ever excavated.

The stratigraphy of the village excavations can be summarized as shallow. The deepest cut, D, went only fifteen inches below the plow zone; Cut A went three inches past the plow zone; Cut B went twelve inches below; Cut C had a total depth of fourteen inches; Cut E was never excavated (or yielded no material); and Cut F was entirely within the plow zone (see Fig. 29). There is no indication that these cuts extended into sterile ground, but that would be the most logical conclusion. Although the village excavations did not extend very deep, the ceramic yield of the six cuts shown in Figure 21 was excellent.

House A.—Despite the conflicting evidence on the extent of the village excavations, the U.S. National Museum catalog, Ford (1936:230), and Vescelius (1957: Fig. 1) agree that they took place in the area east of Mound 2. Sources also agree that an unusual structure known as House A was the most important find of the village excavations.

The first published descriptions of House A are brief. Setzler (1934:38) simply mentions that in the village area they revealed "a rectangular semi-subterranean outline of a house." A confusing description, attributed to correspondence from Ford, substitutes pit dimensions for house dimensions:

> It appears to have been a one-room rectangular house about fifteen feet long and seven feet wide. It was partly undergound, for a clearly marked pit was found in the center. Archaeologists pronounce the house plan very similar to that of the Basket Maker Indians who lived in the Southwest . . . (Ford, 1934:74)

Fortunately, excellent photographs are available to expand these descriptions and Ford (1936:230) offers the following elaboration as well:

> It was small, square in shape, and sunken slightly beneath the old surface of the ground. In the middle of the floor was a square pit with postholes in the corners that extended six feet below the floor of the structure.

Figure 22 is drawn from a copy of the floor plan of House A which was made during the excavations and now is part of an exhibit in the Marksville

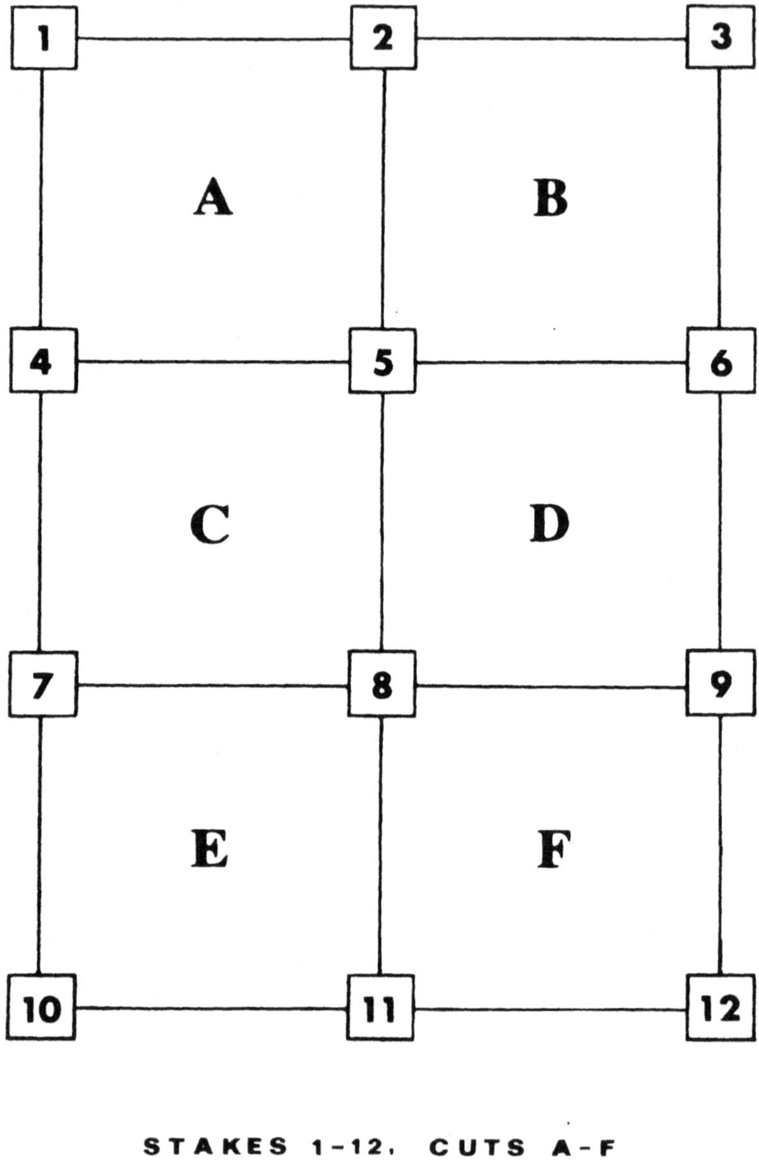

Fig. 21. Marksville village site: schematic plan of escavations.

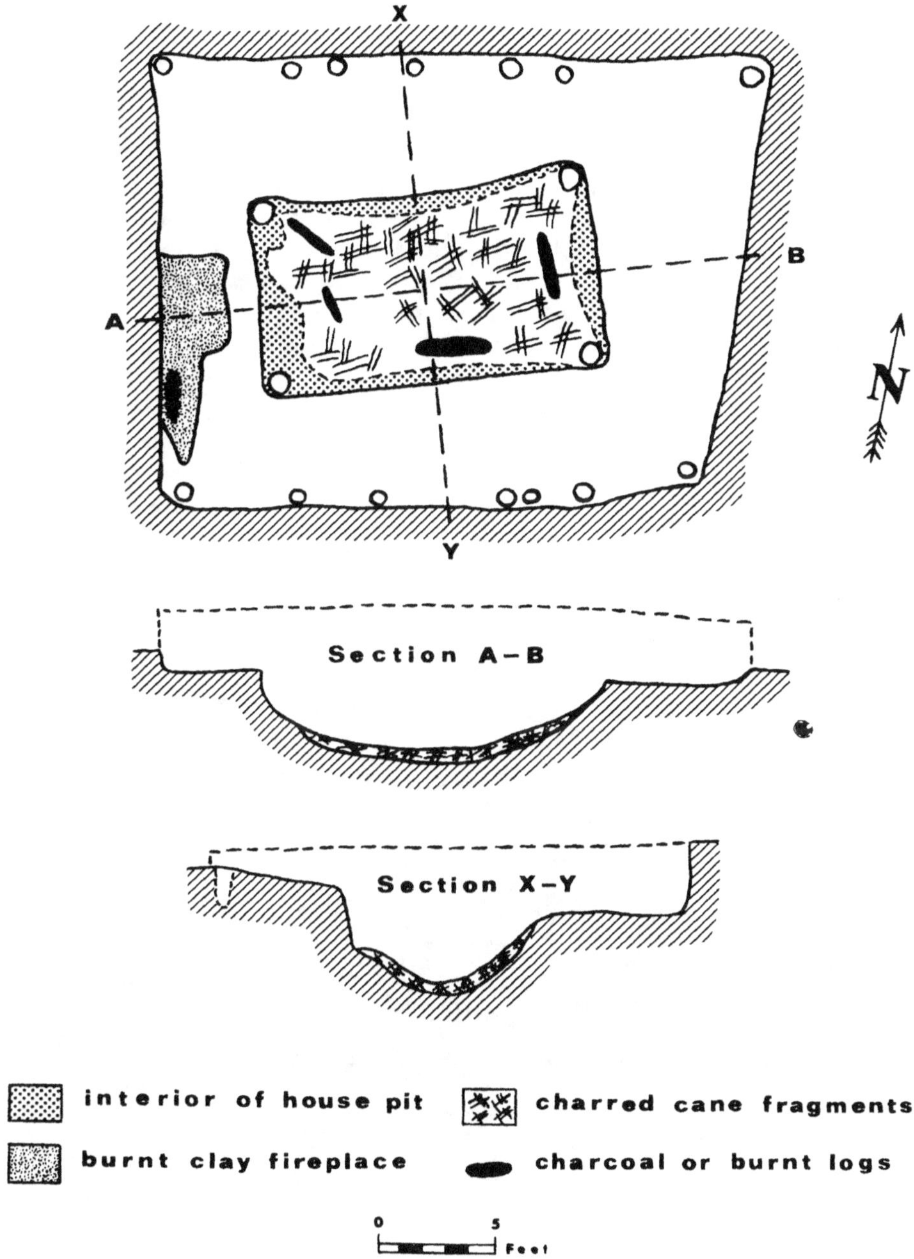

Fig. 22. Marksville House A

Museum. It shows the overall dimensions of the structure to be twenty feet by twenty-five and a half feet. House A was lined on two sides by posts, the holes of which are visible in Figure 23. The men in the picture are troweling out the central pit which measured eight and a half feet by fifteen feet. Figure 24 shows a complete view of House A in which the central pit and side wall postholes are clearly visible. One of the corner postholes in the central pit is visible to the left of the man holding the rod. There is a fireplace on the house floor in front of the same man, but the feature does not show well in this view. In the top portion of the photograph, to the right of the man in the black trousers, is a hole which Setzler identifies as a cache pit.

Vescelius (1957: Fig. 1) shows the exact location of House A in relation to Mound 2. In terms of the provenience recorded in the U.S. National Museum catalog, House A falls within cuts A, B, C, and D (Fig. 21).

The function of House A is an enigma which probably cannot be solved until more excavation is done in the village areas of Marksville and related sites. A great quantity of potsherds was found on the house floor, but it includes ceramic varieties covering virtually the entire temporal range of Marksville ceramics—just as do collections from the surface of the site above and around House A. It would appear that the ceramics represent a deposit of mixed site midden that filled into the house depression rather than the refuse accumulated by House A users.

Fig. 23. House A at Marksville. Postholes outline sides of house, and men are troweling out the central pit. Photograph by Setzler in 1933.

Until more Marksville houses are excavated it would be rash to assume that House A is an example of a Marksville dwelling. The humid Louisiana climate, with an average annual rainfall of 56.7 inches, does little to support such an assumption . A house with a floor situated below ground level, while fine for amphibians and related types, would be highly undesirable for human occupation in southern Louisiana, and hardly what would be expected of a people culturally related to that complex whole known as Hopewell. A more plausible hypothesis would be that House A represents some sort of a ceremonial or public building.

Site X.—Very little can be said about excavations at Site X which was another village area within the main enclosure at Marksville. There is no mention of Site X in the literature, and the only available description comes from a short entry in the U.S. National Museum catalog. Site X is said to be a slightly elevated area east of Mound 6 between the mound and the edge of the bluff. It is uncertain whether Site X is a discrete village location or merely a continuation of the village area east of Mound 2. The catalog records that two cross trenches were excavated to test the area. One of these trenches may be the one shown in Figure 20. A small collection of potsherds and stone artifacts was recovered during the excavations at Site X.

Fig. 24. House A at Marksville. Over-all view of the completed excavation. Photograph by Setzler in 1933.

Excavation by Neitzel and Doran

Louisiana was not excluded from the flurry of archaeology that was spawned by the Works Progress Administration during the 1930s. The LSU-WPA Archaeological Survey in Louisiana was established under the direction of some very energetic and capable men. The overall project supervisor was Gordon R. Willey. Joining him in the laboratory unit in New Orleans was the Research Associate in Archaeology, James A. Ford. In the field, mixed forces of WPA laborers invaded the important Crooks and Greenhouse sites. They were led at Crooks by William T. Mulloy and Arden King; the Greenhouse force was supervised by Robert Stuart Neitzel and Edwin B. Doran. The major aim of the WPA excavations was to untangle the chronology of the Marksville and Coles Creek periods which had been roughly defined by Ford (1936) in a study of surface collections from a preliminary site survey. Excavations got underway in the fall of 1938, and the year to follow must have been an exciting time indeed for those interested in the prehistory of the Lower Mississippi Valley.

Probably because of the previous work by Setzler and Ford, Marksville was not chosen as a prime site for LSU-WPA endeavors. The Crooks site was to furnish the Marksville chronology and Greenhouse the Coles Creek (Ford, 1939). A third site, Baptiste, was excavated also during WPA and it generally was understood by those concerned to fall somewhere in between the Marksville and Coles Creek occupations of the area (Phillips, 1970:896). The Marksville site itself was relegated to the position of an alternate site to be explored only if flood conditions forced abandonment of work at the Greenhouse site.

Just such flooding did cause Neitzel and Doran to move up the bluff to the relative security of the Marksville Prairie in the spring of 1939. The Greenhouse crew was transferred temporarily to the Marksville site where it began digging in the vicinity of Mound 2. Five trenches were opened along the flanks of Mound 2, and the primary objective of these trenches was stratigraphy. Additionally, a small circular depression to the southeast was tested in hopes that it might be another pit house.

Trenches around Mound 2.—The best record of the Neitzel and Doran excavations at Marksville is provided by Vescelius (1957) in an article that was written under Ford's supervision. The material recovered from the Mound 2 trenches is stored at Louisiana State University in Baton Rouge where a catalog is available to provide complete horizontal and vertical information on all the artifacts. Figure 25 illustrates the location of the trenches and is drawn after Vescelius (1957: Fig. 1). The shaded areas represent units from which material in the Louisiana State University collections was taken.

Most of the actual field supervision at Marksville was performed by

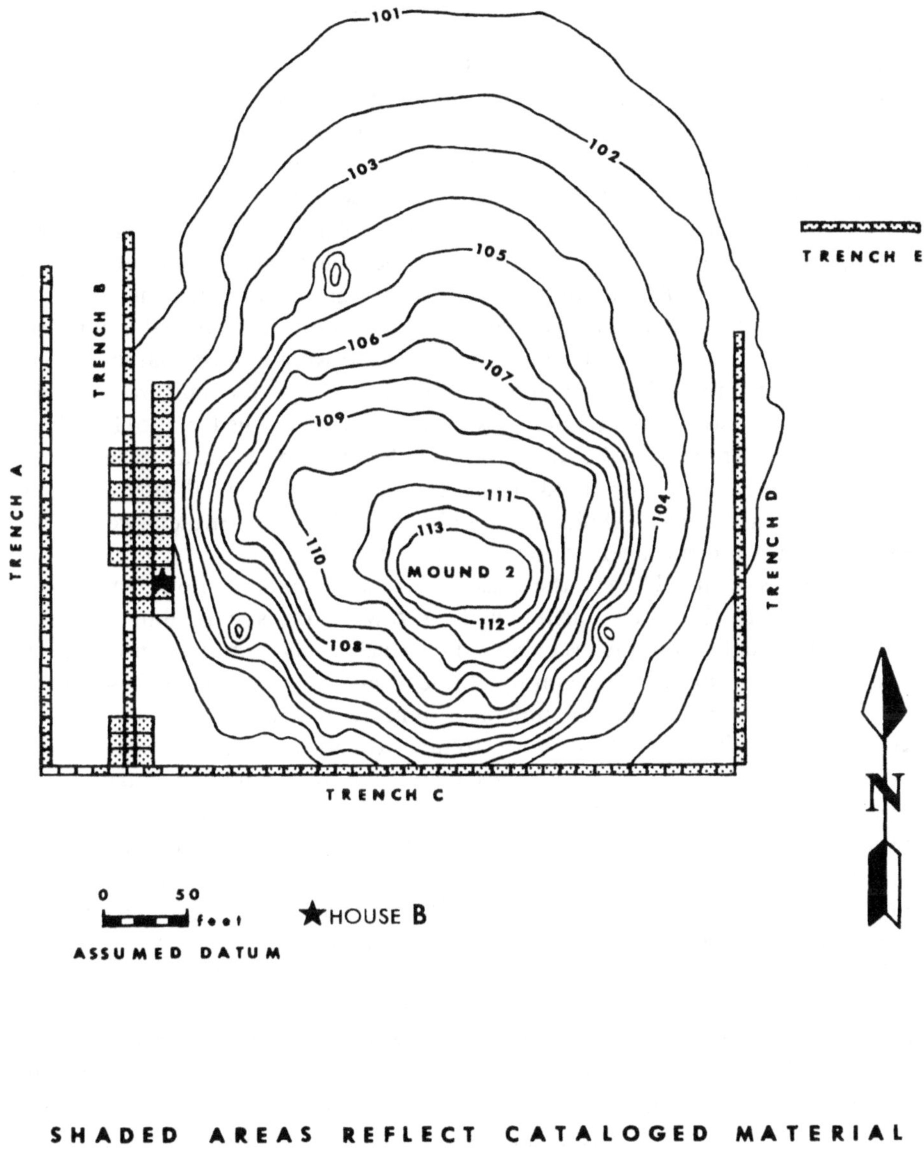

Fig. 25. Trenches around Mound 2.

Doran (Neitzel, October 1973, personal communication). The basic method of excavation was to cut trenches, five feet wide, near the flanks of Mound 2 where it was hoped that material dating the mound had washed down and accumulated in some sort of order. The trenches were taken down in three inch levels, and material from each ten-foot section of the trenches was treated separately. An impressive total of 1,350 feet of trench, five feet wide, was excavated to an average depth of fifteen inches. Additionally, the equivalent of at least 320 feet of trench, ten feet wide, was taken down to a depth averaging eight inches. The total yield of the combined trenches was 6,640 potsherds of which only 17 percent were decorated (Vescelius, 1957).

The trenches differed somewhat in composition but, with the exception of Trench C which cut through part of the mound, all revealed similar site stratigraphy. Under a six-inch layer of plow zone were approximately twenty-two inches of mottled silt which contained most of the cultural material. Other than the two distinct midden strata which Vescelius (1957:418) claims were found in Trench E, the village accumulation appears to have been fairly homogeneous. Beneath the midden was two and a half feet of grey clay-loam which was nearly sterile (Ibid.: 417) and from which no artifacts were saved. Below that was a deep layer of sterile grey clay.

Trenches A and D were the least complicated units. In both, the average depth was only fourteen inches with a few sections extending down to eighteen or twenty-four inches. Many individual levels contained no artifacts. From the standpoint of stratigraphy, these trenches were the least satisfying.

Trench B was the largest unit as a number of cuts, ten feet by ten feet, were added to the central five-foot trench to follow posthole patterns. The central trench averaged eleven inches deep, and the extended squares eight inches. Although postholes were more numerous in Trench B, the site stratigraphy revealed was similar to that found in Trenches A and D.

Trench C cut through a corner of Mound 2 and hence revealed the most complicated stratigraphy. The part of Trench C along level ground averaged sixteen inches in depth, but cuts down to forty-eight inches were necessary in sections that encountered the mound. Three mantles of Mound 2 were exposed above the usual midden layer of mottled silt. It is difficult to relate the vertical and horizontal data in the catalog record to the small-scale profile of Trench C that Vescelius (1957: Fig. 1) provides, but to the extent that this can be accomplished the central portion of Trench C represents the most promising section of the Neitzel and Doran excavations in which to search for meaningful stratigraphy.

Trench E, finally, was the deepest trench from normal ground level. It averaged twenty-two inches in depth with some cuts to thirty inches. Vescelius (1957: Fig. 1) shows two midden strata separated by a thin layer of mottled buff clay-loam. Because of its depth and the possibility of a midden separation, Trench E is another promising unit for studying site stratigraphy.

The case for wall trenches.—Two parallel features which Vescelius (1957:418) identifies as wall trenches were exposed at the base of the plow zone in Trench B. One of these features was followed some forty feet and the other about half that distance. The "wall trenches" were four feet apart, four inches wide, and the "posts" were set at nine inch intervals (Vescelius, 1957:418). Since the features were partially obliterated by plowing, no possibility existed for delineating an overall plan of the building or buildings represented.

An alternative explanation for the parallel features is offered by Neitzel (October 1973, personal communication). He feels that most probably they were made in comparatively modern times by mule-drawn wagons with iron rimmed wheels. Until the state park was established in 1933, Marksville residents frequently visited the site during the wet winter months to cut firewood which they hauled away in precisely the type of wagons that would leave tracks that could be mistaken for wall trenches. The mules' hoofprints in the muddy wheel ruts resulted in the "postholes." In the absence of photographs or other hard evidence pertaining to the parallel features, Neitzel's very plausible hypothesis would seem to leave the case for wall trenches at Marksville highly tenuous at best.

House B.—One of the most important features discovered by Neitzel and Doran at Marksville was "a small, debris-filled rectangular pit house . . . about 10 feet long and 8 feet wide" (Vescelius,1957:418). There are no photographs of House B available for this study, and Vescelius' brief description remains the sole documentation. There was a depression containing a fireplace in the center of house B, and a single posthole was located at each end (Ibid.: 418). Apparently, House B was in a much less perfect state of preservation than House A, and it is likely that the interpretation of House B was influenced heavily by the previous discovery by Setzler and Ford.

Pit house.—The last area tested in 1939 was a circular depression, ringed by an embankment, approximately 350 feet southeast of Mound 2 (Vescelius, 1957:418). Provenience data in the Louisiana State University catalog confirm the location, thereby casting doubt on the obvious assumption that the feature is the Lodge Site 1 shown by Fowke (1928: plate 64) about double this distance southeast of the mound. Ten squares, ten feet on a side, were cut into the feature to an average depth of six inches. One square was taken down to fifteen inches and another to nine. Little was learned about the circular depression; there were no distinct postholes and no fireplace (Vescelius, 1957:418). A small collection of potsherds was the only positive find of the excavations.

Excavation by Ryan

The most recent work at Marksville was conducted by Thomas Ryan in the fall and winter of 1970-71. Assisted by Robert W. Neuman and students from Louisiana State University, Ryan opened a large trench in a doughnut-shaped feature shown as Lodge Site 6 on Fowke's original map (Fowke, 1928: plate 64). Although outside the main earthworks of the site, the ringed depression was considered of interest as a possible house location. The feature, as well as a quantity of other circular soil disfigurations, show clearly on early aerial photographs (Figs. 3 and 4).

Full analysis of Ryan's work has not been completed, and it is not the intention here to present even a preliminary report. Suffice it to say that despite considerable excavation the depression was found to be rather featureless–much the same as in the case of the pit house dug by Neitzel and Doran in 1939. A few isolated postholes were revealed, but they did not seem to fall into any clear pattern. Virtually no artifacts or faunal remains were uncovered. The most surprising find of the excavation was an enormous firepit at a depth of nearly seven feet in roughly the center of the circular feature. Unfortunately, enough charcoal to date the structure was not recovered. The function of the firepit and the purpose of the structure as a whole cannot be conjectured at this time.

II

THE MARKSVILLE SITE COLLECTIONS

A large quantity of excellent ceramic material is available as a result of the major excavations at Marksville. The nature of the sample must be clearly understood, however, for only through such insight can the potential and limitations of the collections be accurately assessed. The difficulty in applying modern archaeological analysis to material amassed to satisfy the more limited aims and objectives of the 1930s should be quickly apparent.

Initially, it can be stated categorically that the ceramic collections from Marksville constitute a non-random sample. The sampling procedure at Marksville, far from being a conscious attempt to objectively sample the entire site as advocated by Binford (1964:427-29), was highly selective. Available material is either from the mounds, in which case it could conceivably represent only mortuary ceramics, or from the most promising village locations as suggested by the distribution of surface debris. Further, excavations were conducted within a normative theoretical framework (Struever, 1971:9-10) which assumed that the portions of the site tested represented the entire site and, moreover, that the artifacts recovered typified all other Marksville sites. It would be a serious mistake to perpetuate such assumptions while re-examining the ceramic material, especially in light of the poor control of the time element that exists at Marksville. It would be equally naive to attempt to apply inductive statistics, or anything more than the most basic descriptive statistics, to such a biased sample.

Accepting the fact that the non-random nature of the Marksville sample precludes a wide range of statistical analyses, the collections might still provide many more invaluable insights to Marksville period ceramics were it not for a far more serious handicap: the extreme dearth of sound contextual data. Such provenience information as exists is extremely general. For the potsherds that were found in the mounds, for example, only mound number is recorded. There is nothing to suggest intra-mound relationships; the analyst cannot know if a sherd was found in the mound fill, on a used mound surface, or associated with one of the burials. Even in the stratigraphic cuts and trenches, for which there is horizontal and vertical provenience, the context is vague. Excavation units consisted of broad, thin slices in which two sherds from the same level might have been found as much as ten feet apart. Profiles that could link finds with specific occupational strata are missing. There is no way to filter out the stratigraphic mixing that might be caused by pits, root molds, animal burrows, erosion, cultivation, and other disruptive factors. In short, one is left with a large ceramic sample within which it is often impossible to determine exact associations between sherds. The lack of contextual data seriously detracts from the information that the collections could provide and fully vindicates the plea of Walter Taylor for recording the complete cultural and geographical record contained within the site:

> A good axiom for archeologists is that 'it is not what you find, but how you find it,' and it is superfluous to point out that 'how you find it' can be told only from notes and not specimens. An archeological find is only as good as the notes upon it . . .. That which is not recorded is most often entirely lost. (Taylor, 1948:154)

The Marksville collections make painfully clear the truth in the above statement and in a more recent expression of the same argument: ". . . context is needed because cultural isolates can neither be understood nor properly used without it" (Taylor, 1972:31).

The possible loss of some potsherds to ceramic type collections is another sample defect which cannot be excluded. It certainly happened in the case of the 1939 material excavated by Neitzel and Doran. A large number of sherds were found in a type collection set up by Ford at Louisiana State University. Sherds in the collection that could be identified by catalog number were used in this study, but it is impossible to determine whether or not all the material was located. Samples may also have been sent to other institutions. One suspects that the same situation may exist in the case of the large Setzler and Ford collection of 1933 for it seems too much of a coincidence that none of the crosshatched rims were joined to decorated body sherds, an association that is not uncommon at other sites or on the whole vessels from Marksville.

Having noted the more serious limitations in the Marksville collections, it is appropriate to acknowledge the potential as well. The collections are substantial and, in the main, the sherds are quite large. There are at least eighteen decorated whole vessels from Marksville on which one can analyze the execution and combinations of decorative treatments, and forty additional decorated vessels from the Crooks site for comparison. There is some provenience information, as well as a general knowledge of the excavations which have taken place at the site. A number of other sites in the Lower Mississippi Valley have yielded controlled material to compare with that from

Marksville. Finally, it must not be forgotten that, despite sample limitations, the collections used in this analysis represent virtually all the ceramics from the site that were obtained by systematic excavation. They are the collections that must be used to define the ceramics of the Marksville phase.

A NOTE ON CERAMIC TYPOLOGY

Any description of a ceramic sample, if it is to be at all structured, must employ some form of classification. Ceramics, like other artifacts which are the product of cultural norms, are best handled by a typological classification which incorporates all possible combinations of attributes on each hierarchical level (Rouse, 1972:54-5). A taxonomic classification, based on mutually exclusive alternates, is unsuitable because the same ceramic attributes may be combined in any number of ways. In simplest terms, a typological classification provides the greatest flexibility in using ceramics to search for meaningful cultural relationships.

The specific typological classification used in this study is well developed for the Lower Mississippi Valley. It is designated the type-variety system of ceramic typology. The most explicit statement of the rules for and the philosophy behind the type-variety system is contained in the important report by Phillips (1970) on the Lower Yazoo Basin. That the classification is designed to express cultural relationships, as well as order the data, is apparent in the following passage by its most successful proponent:

> In other words, the point of view responsible for the classification described in these pages is that types, varieties, and modes are vehicles for the expression of cultural and historical relationships. The emphasis on their formal properties is a matter of prior necessity only because we usually have to formulate these units before we know precisely what the cultural and historical relationships are. (Phillips, 1970:23)

The type-variety system, as described and employed in the Yazoo Basin report, is adopted herein totally and enthusiastically.

There is no need to dwell at length on basic tenets of the type-variety system for they are well defined in the literature both conceptually and by actual usage. However, a brief review of the categories to be used in this study might facilitate an understanding of the emphasis adopted in various areas of the ceramic analysis. The typological units to be employed are type, variety, mode, and treatment. All are discussed in depth by Phillips (1970:23-31). Following the convention established by Phillips (1970:35), variety names will be italicized in the text to distinguish them from type names.

A pottery type is a specific combination of attributes which characterizes a broad class of ceramic manufacture. Types are based primarily on attributes of paste, surface and decorative technique, and as little as possible on form and design (Phillips, 1970:26). When based on decorative treatment, types should reflect a basic decorative idea such as contrasting zones of plain and roughened background outlined by incised lines (Ibid.: 27). Types should be easily sortable, and they need not reflect actual cultural units. It follows that "no limits can be put on the areal and temporal distribution of pottery types" (Loc. cit.).

Ceramic varieties consist of even more specific combinations of attributes which exist within the broader unit of a type. Varieties are not easily sortable because they tend to intergrade. They reflect narrow variations occurring within a type that mirror differences in time or space. Most importantly, varieties must be useful and should not be generated simply to fill out the classification (Ibid.: 27). In other words, because they are created to reflect actual cultural units, varieties must be based on specific variations that can be isolated temporally or areally. Since the Marksville collections are poor in contextual background, extreme caution will be exercised in defining new varieties.

Crosscutting types and varieties are other recurrent attribute combinations which are defined as modes. The relationship of modes to types and varieties is best expressed by Phillips:

> Modes are attributes or attribute combinations that can be usefully employed in investigating and expressing cultural and historical relationships. They are selected out of an endless number of possible combinations to meet specific purposes. In this sense they differ not one whit from types and varieties except that, normally, a smaller number of attributes enter into the combination. (1970:28)

Another important distinction is that while types and varieties are theoretically classes of whole vessels, modes may pertain to specific parts of vessels (Loc. cit.). In this study, for example, attention will be focused primarily on rim and motif modes. It is also possible to define composite vessel modes, conceptually equivalent to "shape," which incorporate a number of individual modes. Tables listing ceramic counts classify by modes as well as types and varieties.

Treatments, finally, are specific combinations of attributes which reflect minor variation in paste and decoration. Treatments are most closely related to varieties and, in fact, they are often based on similar attribute combinations. The main difference between the two typological units is that treatments cannot be tied down to a specific space or time. Often, they can be sorted as well as can varieties, but their utility is subject to question. A treatment is eligible to become a variety if its usefulness—or assumed cultural reality—becomes apparent (Phillips, 1970:29). In analyzing the Marksville collections, great emphasis will be placed on isolating distinct treatments within established varieties in hopes that future excavation and research can be directed toward testing their cultural reality. Towards these ends, the ceramic counts to follow will record in parentheses the frequencies of important treatments that can be identified within established varieties.

As stated at the outset of this discussion, the type-variety system offers the most effective means for searching for cultural and historical relationships. It brings "simplification on the level of type; expansibility on the level of variety; flexibility on both levels" (Phillips, 1970:32). In cultural terms, the type-variety system facilitates the isolation of clusters of site components, defined as archaeological phases, which represent closely related populations that are limited in time and space.[5] Thus, beyond simply ordering ceramic collections, the type-variety system, when used to isolate archaeological phases, "provides a tool toward the eventual identification of prehistoric functioning social systems" (Griffin, 1973:375). Therein lies the objective behind and the justification for the following exercise in ceramic analysis.

MARKSVILLE CERAMIC ANALYSIS

The organizational strategy to be employed in the following assessment of the Marksville collections is, in part, dictated by the nature of the ceramic sample. Since the contextual data necessary for defining new varieties are generally inadequate, the decorated material in the Marksville collections will be described using the types and varieties set forth by Phillips (1970). Special attention is given, however, to ceramic treatments that might be eligible for elevation to variety status. An appendix is also provided in which existing variety descriptions are modified as required in light of the findings from the Marksville study. Such revision is wholly in line with Phillips's concept of the type-variety classification, which represents, above all, a living typology that is specifically designed to be refined as new information becomes available. Before continuing with this chapter, readers who are unfamiliar with the types and varieties of the Marksville period may find it helpful to review the appendix in which appropriate material is described and illustrated.

[5] The way in which archaeological phases, if narrowly defined, correspond to actual socio-political groups is clearly illustrated by the late prehistoric societies encountered in the Lower Mississippi Valley by the De Soto expedition. For a clearer understanding of the phase concept, see Brain et al. (1974) in which there is a discussion of the relationship between the regional cultural phases delineated by Phillips (1970:936-42) for the Mississippi period and the politico-demographic units described in the De Soto narratives. There is so much correspondence between the archaeological phases and De Soto's 'provinces' that the narratives may be used, cautiously, to highlight some of the types of social and political relationships that may have existed between archaeologically-derived phases.

Ceramics from the 1926 excavations

During his three months of field work at Marksville, Fowke uncovered portions of twelve decorated vessels as well as four plain vessels and an undetermined number of potsherds. All of Fowke's material is at the U.S. National Museum. It was not re-examined for this study, but photographs of the whole vessels were sent to supplement the other collections on loan to Louisiana State University.[6] The photographs are the same ones used by Setzler (1933*b*) in his study of Fowke's ceramic finds from Marksville. Setzler's report contains the only descriptive data that are available for the whole vessels excavated by Fowke.

The twelve decorated vessels excavated by Fowke constitute a good introduction to ceramics of the Marksville phase. They are some of the finest examples of Marksville pottery that have been unearthed. The twelve vessels are illustrated in Figures 26 and 27 which were made from the prints supplied by the U.S. National Museum. All the vessels are from Mounds 4 and 8, the two definite conical burial mounds.

The first point that comes to mind when looking at the twelve vessels as a group is that they are all quite small. The largest are only quart-sized, and most range between one cup and one pint in capacity. Statistical analysis of forty decorated vessels from Mound A at the Crooks site reveals a similar situation: 75 percent of the vessels are cup- or pint-sized (Toth, 1973). Large samples of potsherds from the village areas at Marksville give the intuitive impression that greater percentages of quart and multi-quart containers are involved. Thus, small size may be one distinctive feature of Marksville mortuary ceramics.

Despite the small sample size, Fowke's twelve vessels give a fair indication of the diversity in vessel shape that characterizes Marksville ceramics. Small, squat tubby pots (Figs. 26*a* & 27*b*) are probably the most diagnostic Marksville form. They normally have sharply constricted necks, and associated rims may be cambered, vertical, or outslanted. Occasionally, the body bulge polarizes around three or four distinct lobes. In the larger sample from the Crooks site, 32.5 percent of the whole vessels are tubby pots. Figure 26*f* illustrates the very rare combination of the tubby pot with a tapered pedestal base. The only other example was found at the Pharr site in northeastern Mississippi (Bohannon, 1972: Fig. 13*d*).

Small beakers (Fig. 27*a,e*) constitute another popular Marksville vessel mode. Cylindrical in shape, they taper gradually from a maximum diameter at the lip to a minimum diameter at the base. In the Crooks sample, 25 percent of the vessels are small beakers.

[6] The Fowke collections from Marksville have now been examined by the author at the U.S. National Museum, Smithsonian Institution. Analysis of the material closely supports the following general observations except as amended in the footnotes.

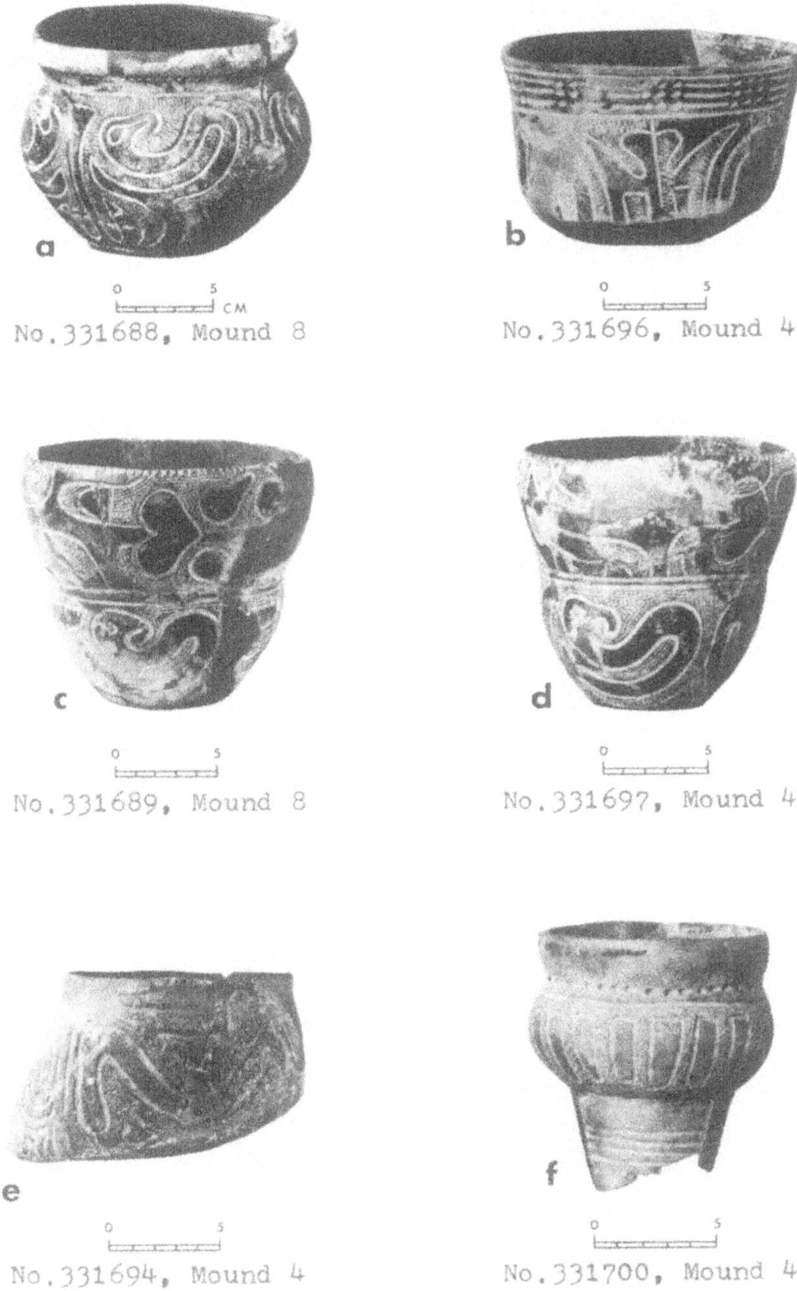

Fig. 26. Vessels excavated by Fowke in 1926.

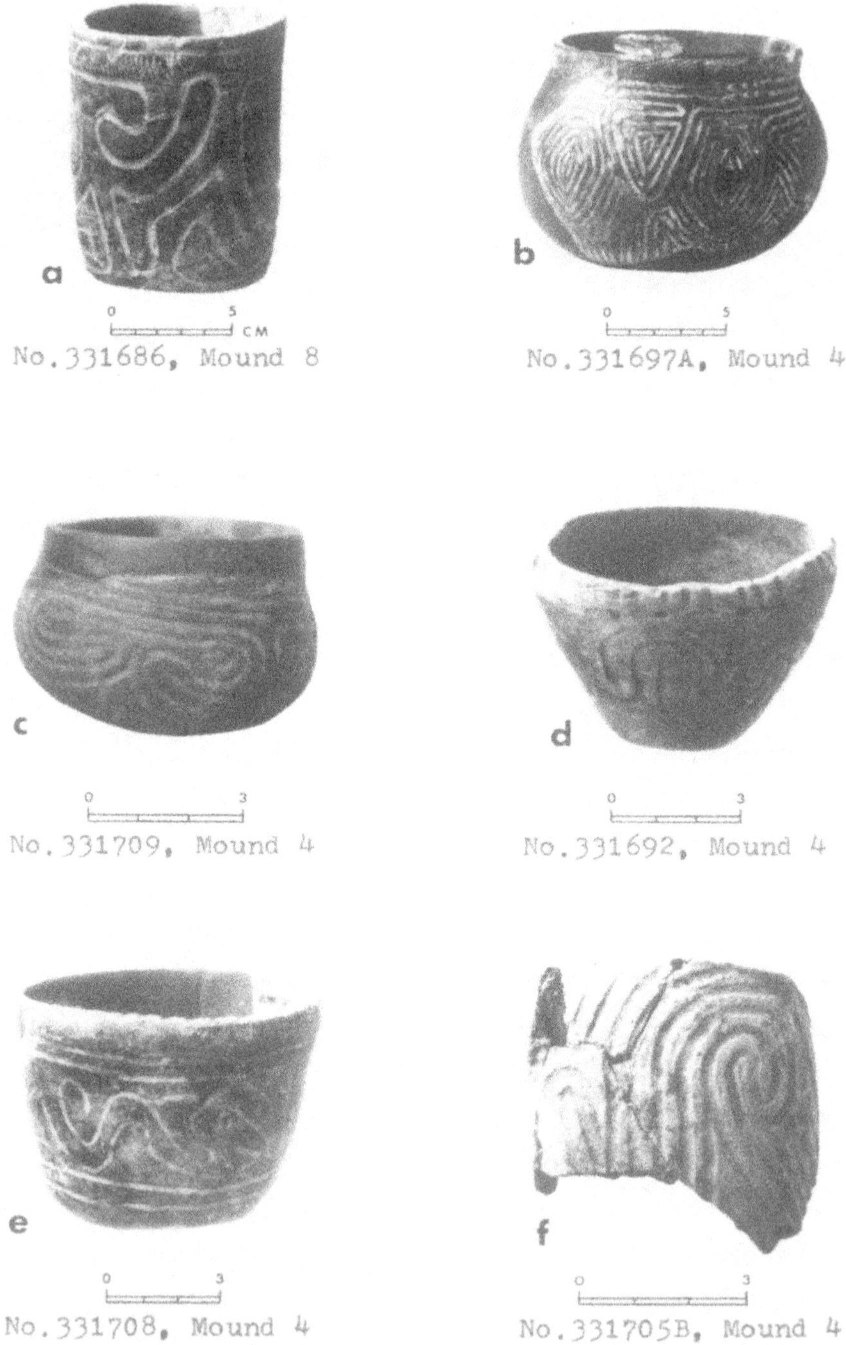

Fig. 27. Vessels excavated by Fowke in 1926.

A third common vessel mode, one that achieves a 17.5 percent frequency at Crooks, is not represented in the Fowke sample from Marksville. It is the straight jar with a slight neck constriction, recurved rim and a maximum diameter midway down the body. The straight jar and additional Marksville phase vessel modes are diagrammed in Figure 28. Except for the bowls, the vessel modes all normally include a flat, usually circular, base.

Following Phillips (1970:28), the "vessel modes" defined for the Marksville phase encompass specific combinations of individual modes pertaining to shape—those involving the rim, shoulder, base, and other structural parts of vessels. The vessel modes in Figure 28 are based on the forty vessels from Crooks as well as those from the Marksville site. The "irregular" category, represented by a boot-shaped vessel form, is not actually a vessel mode but is included as a catchall to handle several shapes which defy classification. Also, Marksville vessels are very often not perfectly symmetrical; many are lopsided, variable in height, or unevenly round.

Judging from Setzler's description of the paste and tempering, the twelve vessels in the Fowke sample are made of the same soft, clay-tempered ware that predominates in the sherd collections from Marksville and at Crooks.[7] The following comments by Setzler (1933*b*:14) apply to the vessels illustrated here as Figure 26*a,b,c,d,f* and Figure 27*a,d,f*:

> The inside surface is rough and has the appearance of small particles of sand protruding; nevertheless these lumps are small pieces of clay consisting either of soft pulverized potsherds or of clay pellets not completely assimilated in the original mixing. The outside surface can be scratched with the finger nail.

Despite the poorly-fired paste and soft surface, some of the vessels are described as having a low polish in places. Again, this is characteristic. The remaining four vessels are said to be made of the same soft, clay-tempered paste but with a harder surface that cannot be scratched without a pointed metal tool. These vessels (see Fig. 26*e* and Fig. 27*b,c,e*) include three that are classified as Marksville Incised, *var. Marksville*. As will be seen, the sherds in the other Marksville collections that have a slightly harder surface tend to be Marksville Incised rather than Marksville Stamped. In sum, Setzler's

[7]The mortuary vessels from Mounds 4 and 8 at Marksville are, in terms of paste attributes, superior to other early ceramics at the site. Although the paste is tempered with medium particles of clay or crushed potsherds as described, many of the vessels are well fired and appreciably harder and thinner than the bulk of the sherds from the village collections. The care that went into the making of the basic fabric of these vessels stands in marked contrast to the situation at the Crooks site where the mortuary vessels—although extremely similar in decoration and form—are predominantly soft, thick, and poorly tempered. Marksville vessels technologically equal to those found in Mounds 4 and 8 are rare in the Lower Valley, but examples are known from the Grand Gulf site (22 Cb 522) in the Natchez Bluff district.

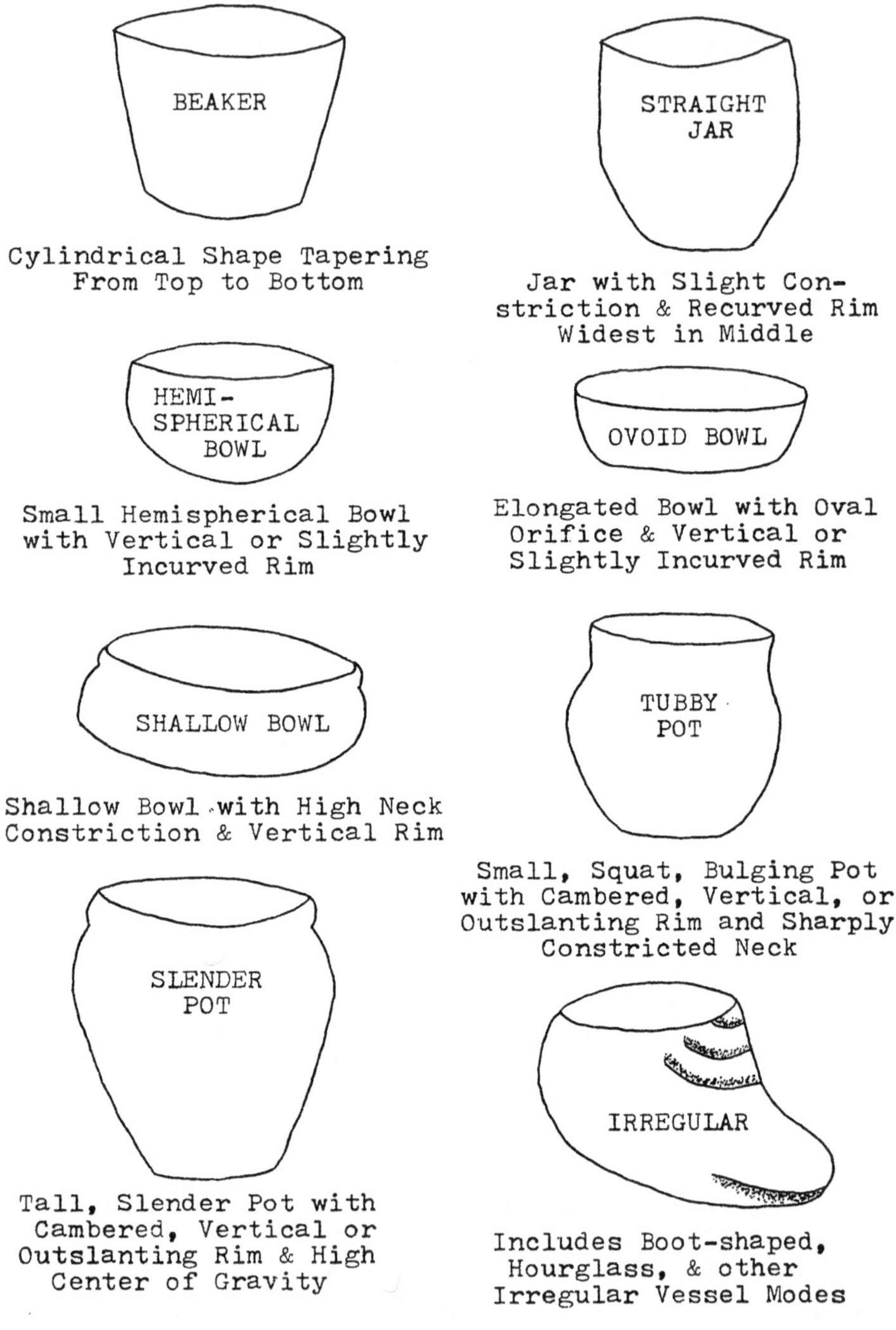

Fig. 28. Marksville Vessel Modes.

description of the paste features of the twelve vessels coincides with observations made for this study on other Marksville samples.

Turning to the decorative aspects of the vessels in Fowke's sample, several very diagnostic Marksville rim treatments are present. The most definitive rim decoration is, of course, the classic Hopewellian crosshatched treatment (Fig. 26*a*). It appears in virtually all ceramic collections attributable to the Marksville phase. A similar treatment involving parallel incised lines that are slanted approximately forty-five degrees to one side (Fig. 27*b*) is another good Marksville indicator. Rim notching, both on top and along the edge of the lip, is also prevalent (Fig. 26*c,d*; Fig. 27*e*). A plain rim band, when set off by a single incised line and sometimes by a row of hemiconical punctates as well, is as distinctive as any of the decorated rims (Fig. 26*f*). The encircling incised line and hemiconical punctates can be combined in a dash-dot treatment that covers the entire rim (Fig. 26*b*) or performs the function of demarcating a distinct rim zone (Fig. 27*b*). All the above rim treatments resemble modes in that they crosscut a number of body decorations and therefore apply to several different types and varieties.

Matching the crosshatched rim treatment as a virtually foolproof diagnostic of the Marksville phase is the well-known raptorial bird design (Fig. 26*a,c,d*). Unfortunately, the design mode is difficult to detect on potsherds because the motif consists of a bird so highly stylized that only the head and a long curved neck are easily recognized. A companion motif, identical except that the bird depicts a broad-billed species, is not represented in the Fowke sample or on any of the other known vessels from Marksville. The broad-billed bird motif is found at Crooks (Ford and Willey, 1940: Figs. 30*b*, 36*e*), and seems to be present on at least two sherds in the Marksville site collections. Most often, the bird design is emphasized by roughening the background with dentate rocker stamping or another equivalent treatment, but on occasion the bird design is simply outlined by incised lines on a plain background as illustrated by vessels from Crooks (Ford and Willey, 1940: Fig. 36*e*), Saline Point (Moore, 1912:499, Fig. 6), and Anderson Landing (Moore, 1908:587, Fig. 4). A final comment on the bird design by Ford and Willey (1940:73) is well worth repeating: "No two are identical and the details frequently change on different sides of the same vessel." The birds portrayed on the two of Fowke's vessels here illustrated as Figure 26*c,d* are about as close an example of replication as can be found. Indeed, the two vessels are so nearly identical in every respect that one can readily support Setzler's conclusion that they were made by the same potter (Setzler, 1933*b*:11). The bird design is known to repeat as many as seven times on the same vessel.

Alternating plain and roughened bands constitute another standard Marksville motif. The bands can be oriented in vertical, horizontal, or V-shaped arrangements. The best example of the alternating bands motif in the Fowke sample is seen on the vessel presented as Figure 26*f*. Equally common motifs consist of parallel meandering lines (Fig. 27*c,f*) or concentric loops (Fig. 27*b*) which are formed by the close-spaced treatment of Marksville Incised, *var. Marksville*. There is also a wide-spaced treatment of the same variety which is used with more open meandering designs (Fig. 27*e*), the bird design, and simple patterns of parallel lines.

A rarer Marksville motif, but one that is very distinctive and easily recognized, consists of heart- and pear-shaped objects (see top portions of vessels shown as Figure 26*c,d*). The design elements also occur at the Crooks site in an arrangement tha looks something like an animal footprint (Ford and Willey, 1940: Fig. 29*b*). Clarence H. Webb (March 1972, personal communication) has suggested that the heart-shaped element may depict a single rattlesnake rattle. Notwithstanding this possible identification, the Marksville heart and pear motif remains to be explained. Meanwhile, it is highly diagnostic and quite useful, for the design elements are small enough to be identified on potsherds.

Another unidentified motif can be seen on the vessel illustrated as Figure 26*b*. Setzler (1933*b*:11) suggests that the unusual design resembles the base of a corner-notched projectile point. Whatever the true identification, the vessel itself is extremely interesting for it embodies a distinctive treatment in which halves of a bisected figure are alternately plain and roughened. The dichotomy immediately evokes a number of possible dualisms: the contrast between life and death, a social organization involving moieties, the opposition of good and evil. However, little can be accomplished by speculating on the possible symbolism contained in this very rare example. More to the point, the alternate treatment deviates from the normal Marksville Stamped, *var. Marksville* practice of roughening the background and leaving the design plain. Phillips (1970:Fig. 359*a*) illustrates an identical treatment with a *Troyville* sherd from the Manny site which presumably has superior paste characteristics and belongs to the Issaquena phase. Perhaps it is a coincidence, but the Marksville vessel in question would appear, solely on the basis of photographs, to be classed also as variety *Troyville*. The possibility is enhanced by Setzler's statement that "the roughening on this vessel is not made with the roulette but by the zigzag technique" (Setzler, 1933*b*:11). The only other vessel which Setzler so describes is the beaker illustrated as Figure 27*a*. It is almost certainly a *Troyville* vessel.[8]

Finally, attention should be drawn to the vessel shown as Figure 27*d*. The poor quality of the photograph precludes detailed comments on either design or decorative treatment. According to Setzler (1933*b*:14), the vessel possesses a simple meandering design delineated against an eroded background of dentate rocker stamping. The tiny pot is noteworthy nonetheless, for it is the one from near the bottom of Mound 4 in which Fowke claimed he found

[8]Vessels 26*b* and 27*a* have been examined and classified as Marksville Stamped, *var. Troyville*. The paste of both vessels points to a Marksville phase association.

remains of maize, squash, and perhaps other forms of food (Fowke, 1928: 420-21). The whereabouts of this incredibly important agricultural evidence is unknown. Griffin (March 1971, personal communication) notes that a search of the U.S. National Museum failed to produce the contents of the vessel, and that Fowke's published statement remains the sole documentation for the possible presence of agriculture in the Marksville phase.[9]

In summary, Fowke's twelve vessels represent a fair sampling of Marksville ceramics. They illustrate a number of Marksville diagnostics such as the crosshatched rim treatment and the raptorial bird motif, as well as some of the major decorative techniques. Nevertheless, there are important omissions: the vertically bisected circle and line-filled triangle motifs; the cord-wrapped stick, straight dentate, and scallop shell stamping treatments; the bowl forms. The foregoing general discussion, however, is not meant to be an all-inclusive description of Marksville ceramics. Rather, the Fowke sample provides a useful introduction to the subject in that it is sometimes best to see how decorative elements and treatments combine on whole vessels before proceeding to a detailed attribute analysis on the level of potsherds. It is in the latter direction that the discussion now turns.

Ceramics from the 1933 excavations

By far the best ceramic sample from Marksville that is available for study is that amassed by Setzler and Ford during the 1933 excavations. As noted previously, although the collection is a fine one, only the most general type of provenience information is available for the 1400 decorated sherds used in this analysis. The 1933 excavations, funded by the Emergency Relief Administration, represent one of the first large-scale projects sponsored by the Federal Government. The success of the Marksville excavations was instrumental in the incorporation of archaeology as a major activity of the Works Progress Administration which was organized in May of 1935. Nevertheless, Setzler (1943:207) admits that he was not accustomed to supervising a large crew of over 100 men. The necessary readjustments and experimentation in archaeological methods spawned by the excessive work force may partially explain the lack of sound contextual data.

In addition to the 1400 decorated sherds from various proveniences within the site, seven decorated and six plain vessels were recovered from Mound 4. The vessels are in the U.S. National Museum and were not available

[9] A more recent, exhaustive search at the U.S. National Museum achieved the same results. There is no record of the plant remains. Smithsonian officials surmise that the remains were sent to their Botany Department for identification, never retrieved, and ultimately discarded. Again, there is no record of such a transaction. It is highly unlikely, therefore, that Fowke's plant remains will ever be relocated to clarify the archaeological record.

for examination.[10] The entire sherd collection, however, was loaned to Louisiana State University where the following observations were recorded.

Surface collections.–Several trends which pertain to all ceramics of the Marksville phase can be recognized in the 1933 surface collections. The first of these sample characteristics is the numerical supremacy of Marksville Stamped, *var. Marksville*. As can be seen in Table 1, the type variety of Marksville Stamped accounts for over half of all the decorated material. Considerable range in the size of the dentate stamp and breadth of the rocker stamping has been allowed for *Marksville* since these attributes seem to be at least partially functional in the sense that they are determined by the size of the zone to be filled. As a working hypothesis, it is speculated that each potter had his or her own stamping tool, more probably a set of them, and that there was no strict requirement for the stamping tools to be of uniform size. None of the *Marksville* sherds in the surface collection are associated with crosshatched rims. Most rims consist of a plain band set off by an incised line, but in a few cases the body decoration continues right to the lip. One rim is notched, and another has dentate rocker stamping on top of a flat lip.

The *Marksville* variety of Marksville Stamped, though it varies in the size and execution of the dentate rocker stamping, has a remarkable homogeneity in paste and thickness. Uniformly, the variety is matched with a very soft paste that is poorly, and perhaps unconsciously, tempered with large particles of what may be either pulverized potsherds or unprepared clay. It is possible that the apparent deficiency in sifting procedures also accounts for the occasional grit that is mixed with the clay tempering. The *Marksville* sherds average 6 to 7 mm in thickness.

Although in photographs some of the *Marksville* sherds might be easily confused with the *Manny* or *Newsome* varieties, the sorting is not so difficult when paste attributes can be assessed by handling the material. The latter varieties are distinguished by a much harder and "cleaner" paste, and tend to be in the range of 4 to 5 mm thick. The paste differences must be temporal rather than geographical, for the *Manny* and *Newsome* varieties can be found in abundance two miles south of Marksville at the Baptiste site. The hard, thin pottery at Baptiste corresponds closely to the Issaquena ceramics from the Yazoo and Tensas regions. Two sherds from the Marksville surface collections were classified as *Manny*, primarily on the basis of the paste attributes mentioned above.

In contrast to the type variety, other varieties of Marksville Stamped show up rarely in the surface collections. Both *Crooks* and *Mabin* are minority decorations and correspond precisely to their published variety descriptions (Phillips, 1970:121-23). All of the *Mabin* sherds embody the cord-wrapped stick treatment. The *Troyville* category is slightly more common, numbering

[10]The Setzler and Ford vessels have been seen by the author during a recent visit to the U.S. National Museum. They complement the Fowke vessels already described.

TABLE 1

CERAMIC COUNTS, MARKSVILLE VILLAGE SURFACE

	RIM	BODY	TOTAL
Marksville Incised			
var. Marksville	9	22	31
close-spaced treatment (18)			
wide-spaced treatment (5)			
line-filled triangle treatment (8)			
var. Yokena	2	1	3
var. unspecified	9	3	12
Marksville Stamped			
var. Marksville	15	117	132
var. Crooks		4	4
var. Mabin	1	2	3
cord-wrapped stick treatment (3)			
var. Troyville	4	16	20
var. Manny	1	1	2
Indian Bay Stamped			
var. unspecified		2	2
Alligator Incised			
var. unspecified	3	1	4
Churupa Punctated			
var. unspecified	2		2
Mulberry Creek Cord Marked			
var. Sevier		2	2
Tchefuncte Incised			
var. Tchefuncte	1		1
Unclassified	3	6	9
Total			227
Diagnostic Modes			
Marksville rims			34
Crosshatched treatment (25)			
vertically incised treatment (2)			
slanted incised treatment (3)			
alternately slanted treatment (4)			
Tchefuncte Plain vessel support			1
"Teat-shaped" leg			
notched rims			5
lines across lip			2
Total			42

twenty sherds. Zoned non-dentate rocker stamping was the sole criterion for *Troyville,* and it should be noted that in paste, rim modes, and thickness these sherds do not differ from variety *Marksville.* In this respect, caution must be exercised in equating the *Troyville* sherds from Marksville with those listed in the Yazoo report (Phillips, 1970) for Issaquena sites. Some of the *Troyville* sherds at Marksville have a slightly harder paste approaching Issaquena quality, but it is difficult to push this distinction very far—especially without better stratigraphic control. At a future date, however, it may be necessary to distinguish two zoned non-dentate rocker stamped varieties on the basis of paste differences. Two unzoned plain rocker stamped sherds having the standard soft Marksville paste are classified as Indian Bay Stamped, *var. unspecified.*

Turning to the type Marksville Incised, a second important characteristic of Marksville ceramics can be gleaned from the surface collections. Specifically, the *Marksville* variety of Marksville Incised is marked by the dichotomy between a close-spaced treatment and a wide-spaced treatment. At Marksville, the wide-spaced treatment accounts for about one sherd in four that are classified as Marksville Incised, *var. Marksville.* As noted in the discussion of Fowke's whole vessels, the two treatments are used for quite different motif and pattern modes. The predominating close-spaced treatment consists of deep, parallel U-shaped lines in curvilinear and rectilinear patterns. The width of the lines is about the same as the space between them. The wide-spaced treatment is used in more open designs, the majority of them involving simple patterns of incised lines.

Most of the rims classified as Marksville Incised, *var. Marksville* reflect a third distinct treatment which is limited to the rim zone: wide-spaced parallel incised lines, normally in a line-filled triangle design. The line-filled triangle both precedes and postdates the Marksville phase: it is common in Tchefuncte Incised (Ford and Quimby, 1945:58); it is found again in the Issaquena *Goose Lake* and *Spanish Fort* varieties; and it continues to be used in the type Alligator Incised. What distinguishes the Marksville version is, of course, the soft clay-tempered Marksville paste already described for the type variety of Marksville Stamped. The broad incised lines are cleanly cut and lack the wet paste incised burr that is common to the Issaquena varieties. Finally, the *Marksville* treatment has, additionally, a strong affinity for the crosshatched and other fine-line Marksville rim treatments.

The paste associated with Marksville Incised, *var. Marksville* is again soft and poorly tempered with clay. There is a slight tendency, however, for the surface to be somewhat harder and less chalky than equivalent varieties of Marksville Stamped. The harder surface, often accompanied by a low polish, is especially prevalent on sherds that constitute well-executed examples of the close-spaced treatment. The harder surface is by no means common to all Marksville Incised, *var. Marksville* sherds; many are just as soft and chalky as the worst Marksville Stamped sherds. The average thickness of both the type varieties is also the same. In much the same way that a few sherds were sorted out as *Manny*, three Marksville Incised sherds were classed as *Yokena* on the basis of harder paste and thinner cross section. All three would be extremely hard to pick out if mixed with an Issaquena collection from the Yazoo or Tensas basins. Similarly, the four sherds sorted, with less confidence, as Alligator Incised, *var. unspecified* would be as compatible with an Issaquena assemblage as with one from Marksville.

The thirty-four Marksville rims are predominantly examples of the fine crosshatched treatment. Five of the rims are incised with parallel lines that are either vertical or slanted to one side at a forty-five degree angle. On several other rims the crosshatching overlaps only at the junction of bands of parallel lines that are alternately slanted right and left. Most of the Marksville rims are flat on top or have lips that slope to the inside. None are really cambered, although a few are slightly thickened. Overall, the most distinctive Marksville rims are rather casually executed and not the best examples of the famous Hopewell rim treatments.

Before concluding the discussion of ceramics from the Setzler and Ford surface collection of 1933, the presence of Tchefuncte material must be acknowledged. Above all, the similarity of the soft, clay-tempered Marksville paste to the Tchefuncte ware described by Ford and Quimby (1945) must not go unnoticed. In summarizing Tchefuncte ceramics, Ford and Quimby (1945:67) conclude that:

> Carelessness in grinding and sifting the clay may account for the presence of large angular lumps which give the appearance of clay tempering to most of the material . . . In characteristics of paste, the pottery in the collections from sites of the Tchefuncte period show two extremes: soft, chalky, ware tempered with angular clay fragments, and ware tempered with a rather large proportion of sand.

The "soft chalky ware," characteristic of the types Tchefuncte Plain, Tchefuncte Incised, and Tchefuncte Stamped, is extremely close to that at Marksville. The sandy ware, as found in Mandeville Plain and the Alexander series, is totally foreign to Marksville ceramics and not one example turned up in the site collections. Another Tchefuncte trait that does appear at Marksville, albeit not abundantly, is a fine clay slip which Ford and Quimby (1945:52,56,58) describe as a common surface finish that frequently is crackled or flaking off. The vessel mode described here as the tubby pot is also the most popular form at Tchefuncte sites except that tetrapodal supports are usually added on the Tchefuncte vessels.

As the description of Marksville ceramics continues, a number of additional parallels with Tchefuncte will be noted. What is important at this point, however, is to make clear at the outset that there is good continuity between Tchefuncte ceramics and those of the Marksville phase—especially in paste attributes. Even though almost all of the decorated material in the surface collection can be accounted for by Marksville types and varieties, there is at least one definite exception: a rim classified as Tchefuncte Incised, *var. Tchefuncte* is decorated in a herringbone treatment that is identical to that illustrated by Ford and Quimby (1945) in their plate 3*q*. Furthermore, the classification of the plain ware from the Marksville site, not attempted in this analysis, would pose a serious challenge. The presence of at least some Tchefuncte Plain is perhaps indicated by the occurrence of a "teat-shaped" vessel leg which matches those described by Ford and Quimby (1945:52). In short, the Marksville surface collection contains a spectrum of related ceramic wares that intergrade from Tchefuncte Plain through the predominant and slightly improved Baytown Plain, *var. Marksville* to a harder and thinner pottery that approaches the Issaquena variety, *Satartia*.

Mound 4.—Several characteristics of the sizeable ceramic sample from Mound 4 distinguish it from the surface collection and the village site collections in general. The unusual features all pertain to the type Marksville Stamped. Most striking, there is not one sherd of the *Troyville* variety from Mound 4 despite the good sample size (Table 2). Although the total lack of *Troyville* must be significant, the reason behind its absence is not easy to explain. One immediate hypothesis might be that *Troyville* is a late variety which postdates the classic Marksville phase and, presumably, the Mound 4 construction. *Troyville* is indeed popular during the Baptiste and Issaquena phases. However, in such contexts it is found with a harder and more compact paste equivalent to the *Satartia* variety of Baytown Plain. Further, a soft, chalky *Troyville* does occur at Marksville in other contexts that contain a full range of early Marksville varieties. For the moment, the hypothesis that *Troyville* is not found in Mound 4 because of a time difference must be rejected as an oversimplified solution.

If *Troyville* is contemporary with the Marksville phase, perhaps it is excluded from Mound 4 for functional reasons. An alternative hypothesis thus follows which maintains that *Troyville* is a utilitarian ceramic decoration which does not enter into the Marksville mortuary complex. In the small collections from Mounds 5 and 6, the lack of *Troyville* lends weak support to the non-mortuary hypothesis. The parallel distribution of cord marking provides the possibility of another exclusively utilitarian decoration. It must be remembered, however, that at least some of the sherds in the Mound 4 collection are supposed to be from midden that was used as construction material (Setzler, 1934:38). Therefore, the sample would be expected to contain utilitarian ceramics. The hypothesis is also refuted by the whole vessels. As already mentioned, a probable *Troyville* vessel (Fig. 26*b*) was found by Fowke in Mound 4—where exactly is not known—and another (Fig.

27*a*) with the burials beneath Mound 8. Further, two more *Troyville* vessels were found in Mound A at Crooks (Ford and Willey, 1940: Fig. 29*c*,*d*). In short, the case for a non-mortuary hypothesis is as unsatisfactory as that for a temporal hypothesis, and the striking lack of *Troyville* sherds in Mound 4 remains unexplained.

Turning to other Marksville Stamped varieties, *Crooks* makes a good showing in Mound 4. In fact, the Mound 4 total of twenty-nine *Crooks* sherds exceeds the combined counts for this variety from all other proveniences at Marksville in the 1933 collection. All the *Crooks* is applied to sherds having a soft, chalky Marksville paste. In general, the size of the shell undulations is

TABLE 2

CERAMIC COUNTS, MARKSVILLE MOUND 4

	RIM	BODY	TOTAL
Marksville Incised			
var. Marksville	17	38	55
close-spaced treatment (39)			
wide-spaced treatment (13)			
line-filled triangle treatment (3)			
var. unspecified	2	2	4
Marksville Stamped			
var. Marksville	13	40	53
var. Crooks	7	22	29
var. Mabin	3	7	10
cord-wrapped stick treatment (7)			
straight dentate treatment (3)			
var. Manny	2	2	4
var. Newsome	1	2	3
Tchefuncte Incised			
var. Tchefuncte	2	1	3
Unclassified	3	7	10
Total			171
Diagnostic Modes			
Marksville rims			13
crosshatched treatment (8)			
vertically incised treatment (2)			
slanted incised treatment (1)			
dash-dot treatment (2)			
notched rim			1
bird design			3
Total			17

matched to the size of the zone to be filled. Several rims have vertical shell stamping on them in a treatment that parallels the very diagnostic vertically incised Marksville rims. Another body sherd has a portion of a flat, typically Marksville, base attached.

Mabin is also more plentiful in Mound 4 than in other units, but the total of only ten sherds is wholly compatible with a previous statement that *Mabin* is definitely a minority decoration at Marksville. Seven of the ten sherds exemplify the cord-wrapped stick treatment, and the other three sherds the straight dentate treatment. One rim sherd has cord-wrapped stick impressions on top of a broad, flat lip. All the *Mabin* sherds are made with a very soft, chalky paste that is tempered with lumps of clay.

A few sherds of *Manny* and *Newsome* are so classified solely on the basis of improved paste and lesser thickness. In paste characteristics and overall delicateness, they clearly stand apart from the remainder of the zoned dentate rocker stamped material which constitutes the *Marksville* variety of Marksville Stamped. The thick, soft, chalky *Marksville* sherds are predominantly decorated by fairly wide zigzags applied with an instrument having medium to large notches. The boldness of the dentate rocker stamping is partly a function of the size of the zone to be filled. Except for the alternate plain and roughened bands motif, all designs are complicated. There are three probable representations of the bird design, and one association with the very bottom of a Marksville rim. Most rims have flat lips that show a strong tendency to slope inward. None of the rims from Mound 4 are markedly cambered. The same rim characteristics are found on the thirteen Marksville rims, which include crosshatched, vertically incised, slanted incised, and dash-dot treatments.

Nearly all of the Marksville Incised sherds are of the *Marksville* variety. The four exceptions, classified as Marksville Incised, *var. unspecified*, consist of very fine incised lines applied fairly casually in complicated curvilinear designs. The Marksville Incised, *var. Marksville* can be divided into the same three treatments found in the surface collection. Predominating is the close-spaced treatment with wide incised lines applied in tight curvilinear and rectilinear patterns of parallel incised lines. The width of the lines is roughly the same as the space between lines. Approximately 25 percent of the *Marksville* sherds display the wide-spaced treatment which is similar in all respects except that the incised lines are used in a more open design. Only three sherds from Mound 4 incorporate the wide-spaced rim treatment that is used with the line-filled triangle motif. Marksville Incised, *var. Marksville* paste is soft and clay-tempered, but again the surface tends to be a little harder, cleaner, and more polished than the Marksville Stamped varieties. None of the Marksville Incised from Mound 4 resemble the Issaquena varieties—the paste and thickness are especially different.

There is, finally, at least a trace of Tchefuncte material in the Mound 4 collection. Precisely how it happened to get into the mound cannot even be guessed because of the lack of specific provenience and contextual data. However, two plain rims certainly fall into the range of Tchefuncte Plain, and three other sherds qualify for Tchefuncte Incised, *var. Tchefuncte.*

In all, the Mound 4 ceramic sample is very similar to the material in the surface collection except that *Crooks* and *Mabin* are more plentiful and *Troyville* is totally lacking. Excluding the three *Newsome* and four *Manny* sherds—and the Tchefuncte material—everything from Mound 4 would seem to reflect ceramics of the Marksville phase.

Mounds 5 and 6.—As can be seen in Table 3, very little ceramic material was found during the Setzler and Ford excavations in Mounds 5 and 6. There

TABLE 3

CERAMIC COUNTS, MARKSVILLE MOUNDS 5 AND 6

MOUND 5	RIM	BODY	TOTAL
Marksville Incised			
var. Marksville	1	2	3
close-spaced treatment (2)			
wide-spaced treatment (1)			
Marksville Stamped			
var. Marksville	2	9	11
Unclassified		1	1
Total			15
Diagnostic Modes			
Marksville rim			1
vertically incised treatment (1)			
Total			1

MOUND 6	RIM	BODY	TOTAL
Marksville Incised			
var. Marksville		2	2
wide-spaced treatment (2)			
var. unspecified	1		1
Marksville Stamped			
var. Marksville		6	6
var. Mabin	1		1
cord-wrapped stick treatment (1)			
Unclassified		1	1
Total			11

is nothing about the type varieties of Marksville Stamped and Marksville Incised from Mound 5 that deviates from the previous discussion of the Mound 4 sample. The absence of *Troyville* should be noted once again. The one Marksville rim is an example of the vertically incised treatment. The two Marksville Stamped, *var. Marksville* rims have dentate rocker stamping right to the lip. In sum, all the material from Mound 5 is diagnostic of the Marksville phase and it would seem plausible that the mound is contemporary with nearby Mound 4.

The Mound 6 ceramics, again, are typical of the Marksville phase. However, there is so little material–all of unknown context–that there is no assurance it dates the mound. The sample could predate the mound as a result of its being included in mound fill, or it could conceivably postdate the structure if the unknown provenience were mound surface. Whatever the case, the *Marksville* varieties of Marksville Stamped and Marksville Incised are similar to material already described. The *Mabin* sherd is an excellent example of cord-wrapped stick impressions placed on a flat lip. There is no *Troyville* nor anything that approaches an Issaquena variety. The one unclassified sherd does not look Marksville–the paste is harder and the three parallel incised lines are narrow, shallow, and clean. Unfortunately, the small Mound 6 collection is most unsatisfying and does little to date the mound or to justify Setzler's designation of a "habitation level."

Village area.–The excavations in the village area between Mound 2 and the bluffs descending to Old River provide the first opportunity to look for stratigraphy at Marksville. Remembering that the exact extent of the village excavations is uncertain, this discussion must be limited to the six cuts recorded in the U.S. National Museum catalog (Fig. 21). In order to evaluate the stratigraphy, it is first necessary to piece together the vertical dimensions of the excavations. Figure 29 reflects the vertical information contained in the catalog record. As can be seen, cuts were not all taken down to the same depth, and levels–here numbered in Arabic numerals–are not constant. The shaded portions of Figure 29 signify levels from which there is cataloged material in the 1933 collection. Whether the blank levels were sterile, or were simply not excavated, cannot be answered. The vertical proveniences are shown for two samples from Cuts B and D that are marked "FROM FLOOR OF HOUSE A." For present purposes, these two samples are combined with a larger collection said to be from "VILLAGE SITE, HOUSE 'A,' FLOOR DEPOSIT." The House A material will be analyzed separately in the next section.

The ceramic counts for the excavated levels of the five cuts from which there is cataloged material are presented in Table 4. At a glance, it is apparent that any possibility of sound stratigraphic information from the Setzler and Ford village cuts is not to be realized. Marksville rims, *Troyville*, and the type varieties of Marksville Stamped and Marksville Incised demonstrate no

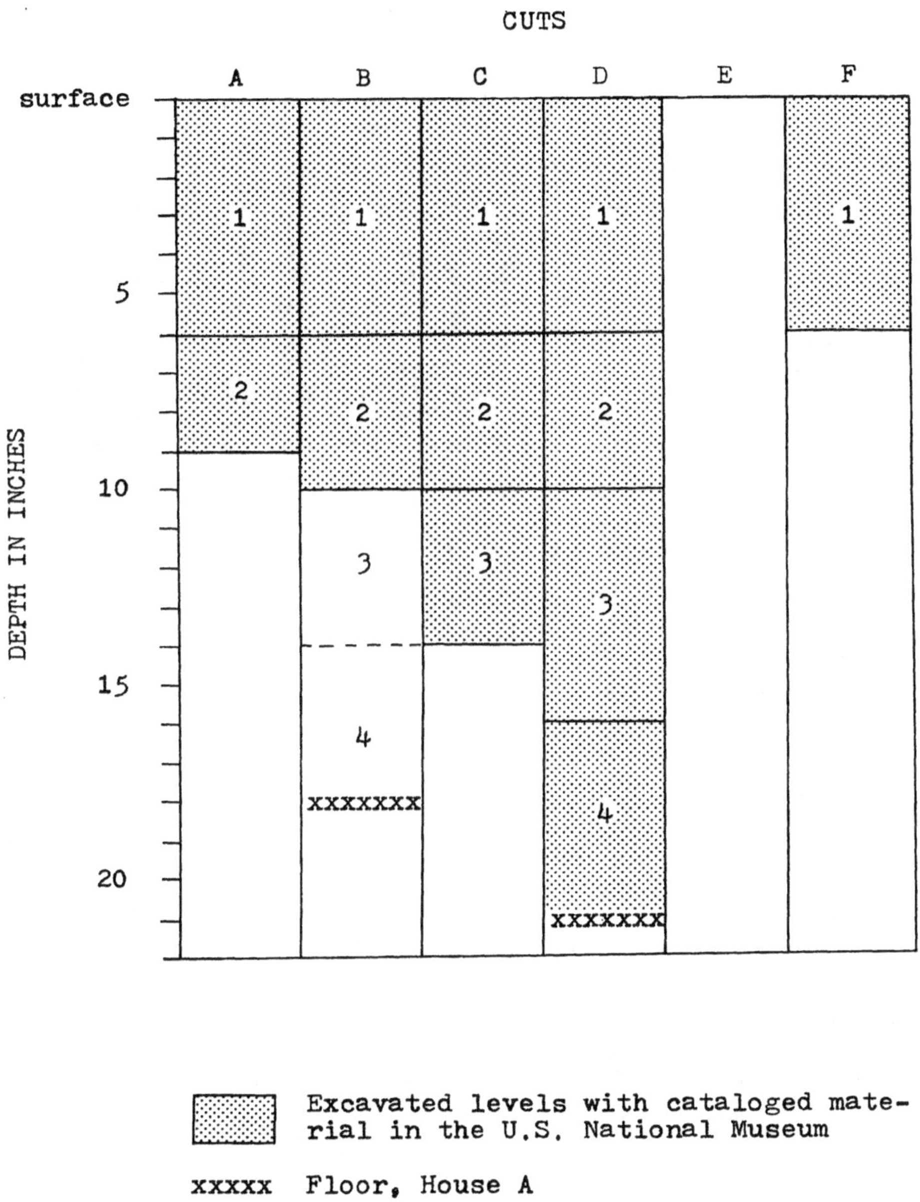

Fig. 29. Marksville village excavations, Setzler & Ford, 1933.

TABLE 4
CERAMIC COUNTS, MARKSVILLE VILLAGE EXCAVATIONS

	LEVEL 1, CUT A	LEVEL 1, CUT B	LEVEL 1, CUT C	LEVEL 1, CUT D	LEVEL 1, CUT F	LEVEL 2, CUT A	LEVEL 2, CUT B	LEVEL 2, CUT C	LEVEL 2, CUT D	LEVEL 3, CUT C	LEVEL 3, CUT D	LEVEL 4, CUT D	TOTAL
Marksville Incised													
var. Marksville	8	6	5	1	2	4	6	3	1	7	3	12	58
close-spaced	(1)	(2)	(3)		(2)	(2)	(4)	(1)	(1)	(3)	(1)	(7)	
wide-spaced	(2)	(3)	(2)			(2)	(1)	(1)		(4)	(1)	(3)	
line-filled	(5)	(1)		(1)			(1)	(1)			(1)	(2)	
var. Yokena				2				2		5		2	11
var. unspecified		2		1		3		3			2	2	13
Marksville Stamped													
var. Marksville	15	16	8	6	3	5	6	14	11	4	14	44	146
var. Crooks						1			1			1	3
var. Mabin				1					2			2	5
cord-wrapped				(1)					(2)			(1)	
straight dent.												(1)	
var. Troyville	5	2	5	3		2	4	2	6	7	7	7	50
var. Manny	1								2		2	4	9
var. Newsome				1				3	2	1	2		9
Alligator Incised													
var. unspecified	1												1
Mulberry Creek CM													
var. Sevier	1		3									1	5
var. unspecified						1						1	2
Unclassified	1							2			2		5
Total	32	26	21	15	5	16	16	29	25	24	32	76	317
Diagnostic Modes													
Marksville rims	3	4	2	2		4	5	2	1	2	1	7	33
crosshatched	(2)	(2)				(4)	(2)		(1)	(2)		(4)	
vertical inc.	(1)		(1)	(1)			(1)						
slanted inc.		(1)					(1)	(1)			(1)	(1)	
alt. slanted							(1)	(1)				(2)	
plain band		(1)	(1)	(1)									
notched rims	1		1	1					1			1	5
lines across lip			1						2				3
Total	4	4	4	3	0	4	5	2	4	2	1	8	41

directional trends in relation to stratigraphic levels. The few examples of *Crooks* and *Mabin* show a slight tendency to be deeper as would be predicted, but *Manny, Newsome,* and *Yokena* also increase with depth which is exactly the reverse of expectations. In short, the stratigraphy in the village excavations appears to reflect a mixed midden situation.

The reason for the jumbled stratigraphy is not difficult to find. House A, which is clearly described as being semi-subterranean (Setzler, 1934:38; Ford, 1936:230), falls within the six cuts. The floor of House A was located approximately twelve inches beneath the plow zone and below the provenience of the sample represented in the ceramic counts of Table 4. Any existing site stratigraphy would have been destroyed when House A was constructed, and, as the house site filled in after abandonment, the overburden would contain a mixture of all previous occupational debris. Such a situation is precisely what is reflected in the Table 4 counts. The greater yield of level 4 in Cut D is very likely a function of its proximity to the floor of House A. The village excavation sample is, therefore, not much better than a surface collection in terms of providing control over the time element at the Marksville site.

Abandoning all hope of stratigraphy, the material from the village excavations still can be useful for comparison with that from the mounds. Comparison of Tables 2 and 4 shows that Marksville Stamped, *var. Marksville* accounts for nearly half of the decorated ceramics in both Mound 4 and the village area. *Troyville*, which is absent in the mounds, becomes very important in the village sample, and cord marking appears as a minority decoration. Issaquena varieties such as *Manny, Newsome,* and *Yokena* also are more abundant in the village area, thus suggesting the presence of a Baptiste phase component in that portion of the site. On the other hand, *Crooks* and *Mabin* are much less prevalent in the village area than in Mound 4. Without better contextual data, it is impossible to assess the real meaning of the above observations of sample differences between the mound and village area collections. At a minimum, the discrepancies would seem to reflect the probability that there were time differences, and perhaps variation in site utilization, within the main enclosure at Marksville.

Measurements recorded for the excavated village sample aid in quantifying intuitive observations on the mean thicknesses of the several varieties present in the Marksville collections. The heaviest sherds are those classified as Marksville Stamped, *var. Marksville*: they average 7 mm in thickness, with a low of 5.5 mm and a high of nearly 1 cm. Marksville Incised, *var. Marksville* also averages 7 mm in thickness, but the variety has a smaller range of only 1 mm on either side of the mean. *Troyville* and *Mabin* sherds average 6 mm in thickness, while *Manny, Newsome,* and *Yokena* all fall between 4 and 5 mm. Surprisingly, the *Crooks* variety averages 4.5 mm in thickness and thus falls well below the range of the other early Marksville varieties. In all, however, there is a clear separation between the early and late varieties. At Marksville, the dividing line is about 5.5 mm with the early varieties thicker and the later varieties thinner. The same division is accompanied by a change in paste attributes: the thicker varieties are made of a soft, poorly tempered ware, and the thinner varieties of a harder pottery approaching the *Satartia* variety of Baytown Plain.

With the exception of *Troyville*, no further description of the village sample is necessary. All other varieties conform to previous descriptions from other provenience units. The excavated village material, however, provides the first large *Troyville* sample and it is appropriate at this point to give the variety a fuller description. *Troyville* is most often found in wide bands, averaging 2 to 3 cm across, which are, in turn, widely separated. The alternating plain and roughened bands motif is predominant, designs being simple and more rectilinear or triangular than curvilinear. Another fairly common motif is the long filled oval. So far as can be ascertained from potsherds, *Troyville* does not seem to be associated with the bird design. Plain rim bands are usually found on *Troyville* sherds; occasionally they are set off by a row of hemiconical punctates. A single incised line, however, is more commonly used to delineate the rim zone. The plain rocker stamping that is used to fill the bands is applied in zigzags that run in a continuous series that parallels the orientation of the band, or, less commonly, in short lengths perpendicular to the zoning lines.

House A.—The ceramic sample from House A is larger than that from any other provenience unit tested by Setzler and Ford. It constitutes nearly 30 percent of the entire 1933 collection.[11] In the last discussion, a hypothesis was presented which stated that the overburden above the floor of House A represents a mixed midden deposit which filled into the house depression after its abandonment. Unfortunately, the ceramic sample from the floor of House A also appears to reflect contamination of the house debris by a mixture of midden which includes nearly all of the varieties present at Marksville (Table 5). It is not possible to isolate the actual occupational remains, and hence the dating of House A becomes a highly uncertain business. It must suffice to compare the floor deposit with other samples from Marksville in a maneuver which is designed to maximize time distinctions.

[11] A sample of 140 additional sherds from the floor of House A was discovered in the course of recent work at the U.S. National Museum. These sherds, inadvertently, were not shipped to Louisiana State University with the remainder of the collection. All of the sherds have zoned dentate rocker stamping. They grade from very soft, chalky Marksville Stamped, *var. Marksville* examples through the entire spectrum of such decoration to the varieties *Manny* and *Newsome*. Time was insufficient for a full analysis of this new material, but enough sherds were sorted to indicate that the sample contained roughly the same percentages of the several varieties as are present in the larger sample discussed below. Thus, the conclusions based on the original analysis still stand. If anything, the new material makes the phase association of House A even more uncertain.

TABLE 5

CERAMIC COUNTS, MARKSVILLE HOUSE A

	RIM	BODY	TOTAL
Marksville Incised			
var. Marksville	31	55	86
close-spaced treatment (40)			
wide-spaced treatment (32)			
line-filled triangle treatment (14)			
var. Yokena	1	7	8
var. Leist	1	3	4
var. Spanish Fort	1		1
var. unspecified	8	11	19
Marksville Stamped			
var. Marksville	23	61	84
var. Crooks		7	7
var. Mabin	3	3	6
cord-wrapped stick treatment (4)			
straight dentate treatment (2)			
var. Troyville	16	65	81
var. Manny	9	4	13
var. Newsome	4	5	9
var. unspecified		5	5
Alligator Incised			
var. unspecified		4	4
Mulberry Creek Cord Marked			
var. Sevier	1	8	9
var. unspecified	1	1	2
Catahoula Zoned Red			
var. Catahoula		1	1
Unclassified	4	9	13
Total			352
Diagnostic Modes			
Marksville rims			32
crosshatched treatment (15)			
vertically incised treatment (3)			
slanted incised treatment (4)			
alternately slanted treatment (10)			
notched rims			10
lines across lip			7
bird design			1
Total			50

To begin, the contents of the overburden above the House A floor should contain the most important comparisons for assessing the time frame in which the house depression was filled. Like the House A floor sample, the overburden contains a mixture of early Marksville and late Marksville ceramics. Stated differently, both samples indicate that components of the Marksville and Baptiste phases are represented. To exploit this possibility, the ceramic counts of Tables 4 and 5 can be pared down to the most diagnostic varieties. For the Marksville phase, the most foolproof markers are *Crooks, Mabin,* and the Marksville rims; for the Baptiste phase, *Yokena, Leist, Spanish Fort, Manny,* and *Newsome* are the most definitive.

Using only the marker varieties, the sample differences become accentuated. Marksville phase markers maintain the same percentage in the overburden and the floor deposit, constituting 12.9 and 12.8 percent of the total samples respectively. Baptiste phase markers, however, are slightly more concentrated on the house floor where they achieve 11.1 percent frequency as opposed to 9.4 percent in the overburden. Further, *Troyville* is found at a 23.0 percent level on the house floor and only a 15.8 percent level in the overburden. Unfortunately, during the analysis *Troyville* was not sorted into soft/thick and hard/thin categories—both of which are present—and thus probably relates to both phases. It is significant, however, that *Troyville* is more abundant by far on the floor of House A than anywhere else at Marksville. Combined with the consistency of Marksville phase markers and an increase of Baptiste phase markers on the house floor, the *Troyville* density does not seem compatible with a situation in which a Marksville house was filled with contemporary and later midden. Rather, the better hypothesis would be that a Baptiste phase house was filled by surrounding earlier Marksville midden and contemporary Baptiste refuse. The best test of the hypothesis was missed when the charred logs and burnt cane found in the house pit were innocently discarded. As stated at the outset, the dating of House A remains very speculative.

Before turning to a few descriptive comments on the house floor ceramics, a brief comparison of this sample with that from other proveniences at Marksville can be made. The ratio of the type varieties ot Marksville Incised and Marksville Stamped provides some interesting insights when followed across the site. In the surface collection and in the excavated village cuts Marksville Stamped, *var. Marksville* comprises roughly half of the decorated material. The ratio of the type varieties is 31 incised/132 stamped in the surface collections and 58 incised/146 stamped in the village cuts. In Mound 4 and House A, however, the ratio of the type varieties becomes almost even: 55 incised/53 stamped in Mound 4 and 86 incised/84 stamped on the floor of House A.[12] The reduction in the supremacy of Marksville Stamped, *var. Marksville* is, in part, compensated for by an increase in other Marksville Stamped varieties.

[12]The new material from the floor of House A contradicts this statement as there is now substantially more Marksville Stamped, *var. Marksville* to be reckoned with from House A. The observation is still true as it pertains to Mound 4.

Crooks and *Mabin* gain at the expense of *Marksville* in Mound 4, and *Troyville* equals the type variety in House A. Once again, the dichotomy of *Crooks* and *Mabin* in Mound 4 and *Troyville* in House A seems to bespeak important function or time differences at Marksville. For the present, the sharp sample differences lend weak support to the hypothesis that Mound 4 and House A are not coeval.

Recognition of a Baptiste component in the House A floor sample depends on the ability to distinguish Issaquena varieties from those of the Marksville phase. In the case of the House A sample, the sorting is facilitated by rather distinctive paste differences, some of which have been mentioned previously in other contexts.[13] *Manny* and *Newsome* are so classified because the representative sherds are significantly better tempered, harder, cleaner, and thinner than examples of the type variety. Execution of the dentate rocker stamping is often much neater on the *Manny* and *Newsome* sherds, but this is a point that should not be pushed very far. *Troyville* includes combinations of paste attributes comparable to both the *Manny/Newsome* ware and the *Marksville* ware. The variety should have been subdivided along these lines, but the paste differences—although noted—were not recognized as important at the time of analysis. The hard paste and soft paste *Troyville* distinction does not seem to be accompanied by differences in design or execution.

The Marksville Incised varieties *Yokena* and *Leist* are again based partially on paste attributes, but design and rim modes also enter into the classification. The "Two-line Circle" mode (Phillips, 1970:118) is found in the *Yokena* at Marksville, and the tight concentric loops, or "fingerprint," design that is typical of *Leist* is present as well. With a Baptiste component reflected in the House A sample, some of the Marksville Incised, *var. Marksville*, line-filled triangle treatment could easily be *Goose Lake* or *Spanish Fort*. However, the *Marksville* classification was retained because the sherds have the soft Marksville paste rather than the *Satartia* paste required for *Goose Lake*, and the wet-paste incised burr characteristic of *Spanish Fort* is normally lacking. One sherd that did show some burr and had a paste approaching *Reed* was finally typed as *Spanish Fort*. As to thickness, the *Leist* averaged 4 mm, the *Spanish Fort* sherd was 7 mm, and the *Marksville* held to its normal average of 7 mm.

Finally, the Marksville Stamped, *var. Marksville* from the floor of House A resembles that from the overburden in that designs are not very complex. Most popular motifs would seem to include concentric circles—not bisected—and wide meandering loops. The bird design, if present, is not obvious. The single identifiable occurrence of the bird motif was on a *Crooks* sherd. One *Marksville* rim was deeply notched.

[13]Some sherds in the new sample from House A are extremely hard to classify because the paste falls midway between that of the Marksville and Baptiste phases. Although frustrating, this is a good indication of the continuity in Marksville period ceramics.

In summary, House A ceramics include a typical spectrum of Marksville phase pottery although the proportions of several varieties, such as *Troyville*, are in some ways deviant. The House A ceramics also provide the best assortment of Issaquena varieties which, on the Marksville Prairie, signify a component of the Baptiste phase (Phillips, 1970:897). Large as the sample is, the House A floor deposit cannot be sufficiently separated to securely date the structure. The most reasonable guess is that House A was possibly used at or until a time that postdates the construction of the burial mounds at the site.

Site X.—A slightly elevated stretch of ground east of Mound 6 has been given the rather ambiguous name of "Site X." It is uncertain whether or not this is a discrete occupational locus within the Marksville site or simply a continuation of the village area adjacent to Mound 2. In any case, the U.S. National Museum catalog indicates that two cross trenches were excavated at Site X, and a small ceramic sample resulted from the endeavor. There is no vertical or horizontal provenience for the collection.

The Site X ceramics, summarized in Table 6, can be characterized quite briefly. The type varieties of both Marksville Stamped and Marksville Incised are the same as those described previously for other proveniences within the

TABLE 6

CERAMIC COUNTS, SITE X

	RIM	BODY	TOTAL
Marksville Incised			
var. Marksville	1	14	15
close-spaced treatment (8)			
wide-spaced treatment (6)			
line-filled triangle treatment (1)			
var. unspecified		4	4
Marksville Stamped			
var. Marksville	3	24	27
var. Crooks		1	1
Unclassified		1	1
Total			48
Diagnostic Modes			
Marksville rims			7
crosshatched treatment (5)			
slanted incised treatment (1)			
alternately slanted treatment (1)			
Total			7

site. One large Marksville Stamped, *var. Marksville* sherd is an excellent example of the concentric circle motif. There is no *Troyville* in the collection. One Marksville Incised, *var. unspecified* sherd is noteworthy because it embodies a treatment which occurs in extremely small frequencies in other samples. The trace decoration consists of zones outlined by normal wide U-shaped lines and filled with unusually narrow, close-spaced, parallel incised lines. The treatment is reminiscent of the *Laborde* variety of French Fork Incised, but its Marksville identity is assured by the soft, chalky paste and, in this instance, a row of hemiconical punctates. In all, Site X ceramics are typical of the Marksville phase and would seem to indicate that this portion of the site was utilized during the period of burial mound construction.

Village miscellaneous.—The final ceramic sample in the Setzler and Ford collection lacks specific provenience except that it is said to come from the village area. In view of all the foregoing discussions, very little descriptive detail can be added without being repetitive. The content of the miscellaneous village sample is presented in Table 7. As can be seen, the sample closely resembles the surface collection with varieties of the Marksville phase strongly predominating over those of the Baptiste phase.

Marksville Stamped, *var. Marksville* accounts for just over half of the total decorated, as in the case of the surface collection. In general, the type variety is characterized by rather bold rocker stamping that is applied by an instrument with medium to large notches. The soft paste, tempered with large particles of clay, often results in a heavily eroded, worn surface on which the dentate rocker stamping is partially obliterated. Analysis of the *Marksville* sherds from the village area does not leave one with the impression that the bird design is prevalent. In fact, other motifs such as concentric circles can be detected in much greater frequencies.

Most Marksville Stamped, *var. Marksville* rim sherds show the body design continuing right to the lip or stopping at a plain narrow rim band, and there is only one example in the entire 1933 collection of the type variety associated with the base of a Marksville rim. The non-association of Marksville rims and Marksville Stamped, *var. Marksville* is, perhaps, a function of vessel form: the rims classified as *Marksville* are normally from straight jars or beakers while the Marksville rims are from tubby pots. The sharply constricted neck of the tubby pot may result in a weak zone along which breakage is common, thus separating the Marksville rims from *Marksville* bodies.

The village miscellaneous sample contains a large assortment of Marksville rims, thus permitting a few final comments on this very diagnostic mode. Most of the Marksville rims are vertical or outslanted rather than cambered, and there is a strong tendency for the lips to be flat or slightly slanted to the inside of the vessel. When a Marksville rim is cambered, the lip has a tendency to be more rounded. Many Marksville rims have very fine-line crosshatching, and these rims almost always have a row of hemiconical punctates underneath

TABLE 7

CERAMIC COUNTS, VILLAGE MISCELLANEOUS

	RIM	BODY	TOTAL
Marksville Incised			
var. Marksville	9	7	16
close-spaced treatment (3)			
wide-spaced treatment (5)			
line-filled triangle treatment (8)			
var. Leist	1	1	2
var. unspecified		1	1
Marksville Stamped			
var. Marksville	13	35	48
var. Crooks	2	4	6
var. Mabin	1		1
cord-wrapped stick treatment (1)			
var. Troyville	1	3	4
var. Manny	1	3	4
var. Newsome	1	2	3
Unclassified		1	1
Total			86
Diagnostic Modes			
Marksville rims			28
crosshatched treatment (16)			
vertically incised treatment (2)			
slanted incised treatment (2)			
alternately slanted treatment (8)			
lines across lip			3
Total			31

the decoration. Other rims, however, have rather wide incising with considerable burr where the lines cross. A presently untestable hypothesis is that the cambered rims with rounded lips and fine-line crosshatching are slightly earlier than the straight rims with flat lips and poorly executed crosshatching. There are many parallel situations in Lower Valley ceramics where a treatment degenerates toward the end of its time—the *Mazique* to *Kings Point* to *Manchac* sequence is a good case in point (see, for example, Phillips, 1970:129-30).

As usual, varieties characteristic of the Baptiste phase are distinguished by a harder paste and lesser thickness. The *Leist, Manny,* and *Newsome* all range between 4 and 5 mm in thickness in contrast to the 6 to 8 mm range of the Marksville phase varieties. While some sherds did exhibit paste attributes that intergrade between the soft and hard wares, all those classified as late varieties are rather clear-cut examples of the improved paste. The Baptiste phase varieties, along with *Crooks, Mabin,* and *Troyville*, are minority decorations in the village miscellaneous collection.

Summary.—The foregoing pages endeavored to describe the Setzler and Ford ceramic collection from Marksville, the content of which is summarized in Table 8. Although the discussion has often mired in ceramic minutiae, several general themes were developed in passing. Common to all of the hpotheses is the belief that there is a fairly extensive time depth represented in the main enclosure at Marksville. The ceramic analysis indicated that at least three components are involved: Tchefuncte, Marksville, and Baptiste. A fourth component, one obviously not amenable to ceramic study, is also possible, for early projectile points, baked clay balls, and hematite plummets demonstrate the presence of a Poverty Point phase on the eastern margin of the Marksville Prairie. A fitting conclusion to the description of the 1933 collection is, then, an interim review of the evidence relating to the three identifiable components.

Most of the 1400 decorated potsherds in the Setzler and Ford collection can be classified as Marksville types and varieties. However, a few sherds of Tchefuncte Incised, *var. Tchefuncte* are present and must be included in the ceramic counts. It should also be acknowledged that a number of Marksville treatments and motifs have Tchefuncte prototypes: notched rims, plain rocker stamping, line-filled triangles, and even the slanted incised and crosshatched rims (see Ford and Quimby, 1945: Plates *2a,h* and *3h,i,j*). Perhaps more meaningful than the decorative similarities is the apparent continuity between Tchefuncte Plain, *var. Tchefuncte* and Baytown Plain, *var. Marksville*. A soft, poorly fired paste that is tempered—perhaps unconsciously—by large particles of clay links the ceramics of the Tchefuncte and Marksville phases on the Marksville Prairie. A continuum of paste characteristics can be detected in the 1933 collection which suggests a gradual improvement in pottery manufacture during the centuries of site occupation. The continuity of ceramic wares leads to a hypothetical model in which the decorative elements of Hopewellian pottery are introduced to and incorporated by a resident Tchefuncte population. The similarity of Marksville and Tchefuncte paste, and the occasional errors in replication of Hopewellian motifs, are not indicative of the alternative possibility, namely full site-unit intrusion.

Ceramics indicate that the main occupation of the Marksville site was during the classic Marksville phase, which probably dates within the time frame of 100 B.C. to A.D. 200. The type varieties of Marksville Stamped and Marksville Incised predominate in all samples. *Crooks, Mabin,* and the Marksville rims join the type varieties as highly diagnostic phase markers. All Marksville phase ceramics are associated with a soft, clay-tempered paste which intergrades between the plain wares of the Tchefuncte and Baptiste phases. Most sherds attributable to the Marksville phase are between 6 and

TABLE 8

CERAMIC SUMMARY, 1933 COLLECTION

	MOUND 4	MOUND 5	MOUND 6	SURFACE	LEVEL 1	LEVEL 2	LEVEL 3	LEVEL 4	HOUSE A	SITE X	MISC.	TOTAL
Marksville Incised												
var. Marksville	55	3	2	31	22	14	10	12	86	15	16	266
var. Yokena				3	2	2	5	2	8			22
var. Leist									4		2	6
var. Spanish Fort									1			1
var. unspecified	4		1	12	3	6	2	2	19	4	1	54
Marksville Stamped												
var. Marksville	53	11	6	132	48	36	18	44	84	27	48	507
var. Crooks	29			4		2		1	7	1	6	50
var. Mabin	10		1	3	1	2		2	6		1	26
var. Troyville				20	15	14	14	7	81		4	155
var. Manny	4			2	1	2	2	4	13		4	32
var. Newsome	3				1	5	3		9		3	24
var. unspecified									5			5
Catahoula Zoned Red												
var. Catahoula									1			1
Indian Bay Stamped												
var. unspecified				2								2
Mulberry Creek CM												
var. Sevier				2	4			1	9			16
var. unspecified						1		1	2			4
Alligator Incised												
var. unspecified				4	1				4			9
Churupa Punctated												
var. unspecified				2								2
Tchefuncte Incised												
var. Tchefuncte	3			1								4
Unclassified	10	1	1	9	1	2	2		13	1	1	41
Total	171	15	11	227	99	86	56	76	352	48	86	1227
Diagnostic Modes												
Marksville rims	13	1		34	11	12	3	7	32	7	28	148
crosshatched	(8)			(25)	(4)	(7)	(2)	(4)	(15)	(5)	(16)	
vertically inc.	(2)	(1)		(2)	(3)	(1)			(3)		(2)	
slanted inc.	(1)			(3)	(1)	(2)	(1)	(1)	(4)	(1)	(2)	
alt. slanted				(4)		(2)		(2)	(10)	(1)	(8)	
dash-dot	(2)											
plainband					(3)							
bird design	3								1			4
notched rims	1			5	3	1		1	10			21
lines across lip				2	1	2			7		3	15
Total	17	1	0	41	15	15	3	8	50	7	31	188

8 mm in thickness, with a small proportion going as high as a centimeter. A soft, thick *Troyville* is apparently part of the Marksville phase ceramic complex, but, inexplicably, *Troyville* sherds are not present in the mound collections of Setzler and Ford. Overall, Marksville phase ceramics, despite a humble paste, are well-decorated with an assortment of sophisticated designs that relate closely to the pottery of northern Hopewell.

Returning to a broader level of analysis, the Setzler and Ford collection provides further illustration of the way ceramic attributes are combined on whole vessels. Figure 30 represents a partial photographic record of the whole vessels found in Mound 4 during the 1933 excavations. In all, seven decorated and six plain vessels were recovered. They exemplify a number of familiar Marksville phase treatments, modes, and motifs. Deeply notched lips can be seen on the vessels presented as Figure 30*a,e*. The open, meandering band design on vessel 30*a* employs the boldly rocked, large dentate stamp treatment which is common for Marksville Stamped, *var. Marksville*. Vessels 30*c* and 30*d* illustrate respectively the wide-spaced and close-spaced treatments of Marksville Incised, *var. Marksville*. Any doubts about the contemporaneity of the type varieties of Marksville Stamped and Marksville Incised are dispelled forever by vessel 30*b* which combines both decorations on one pot. Several sherds in the 1933 collection attest to the fact that the combination of a close-spaced Marksville Incised, *var. Marksville* design with a Marksville Stamped, *var. Marksville* design is not limited solely to vessel 30*b*. Finally, a plain vessel, 30*f*, is included to show the characteristic lopsided, non-symmetrical quality of Marksville ceramic manufacture.

A component of the Baptiste phase is represented in the Marksville site collections by a small percentage of pottery that is distinctively harder, better tempered, and thinner than the rest. The compact paste, similar to the *Satartia* variety of Baytown Plain, is found in *Manny, Newsome, Yokena*, and other varieties diagnostic of the Baptiste phase. Some *Troyville* having the same improved paste seems to go with the Baptiste ceramic complex, but in the analysis it was not distinguished from the *Troyville* with a softer Marksville paste. Given the general provenience of the Setzler and Ford collection, it is not possible to isolate the sources of the Baptiste ceramics within the Marksville site. However, the greater frequencies of the late Marksville varieties on the floor of House A might indicate that the village area east of Mound 2 is at least one locus of Baptiste phase occupation.

Concerning the relative dating of site features at Marksville, the 1933 collections offer little firm evidence for speculation. The samples from Mounds 4 and 5 are compatible with the notion that the burial mounds were erected during the Marksville phase. Mounds 2, 3, and 6 remain undated as does the semicircular embankment known as Enclosure A. In hopes of achieving a better chronological perspective for the Marksville site, the discussion now turns to the material acquired by Neitzel and Doran in 1939 as

Fig. 30. Vessels excavated by Setzler & Ford in 1933.

the result of excavations purposely directed to the examination of site stratigraphy.

Ceramics from the 1939 excavations

The lack of sound chronological data from the Setzler and Ford excavations at Marksville was realized by the investigators, and the Greenhouse crew directed by Neitzel and Doran was temporarily assigned to Marksville with the explicit aim of correcting the deficiency. Material from the trenches around Mound 2, therefore, is of great importance for it represents the last available sample that might reveal clear site stratigraphy. Since the 1939 ceramics closely resemble those already described, descriptive comments will be limited in this section, in favor of increased focus on the chronological aspects of the excavations.

Vertical and horizontal provenience is known for every sherd in the Neitzel and Doran collection. However, profiles of the trenches, needed to tie the vertical provenience with site stratigraphy, cannot be located. Neitzel (November 1973, personal communication) is sure that the profiles were drawn, and Vescelius (1957) wrote as if some of them were available to him. Unfortunately, profiles are lacking except for the two small-scale sections of Trenches C and E that are illustrated by Vescelius (1957: Fig. 1), so that the present study is severely handicapped in all attempts to extract meaningful chronology from the collections.

Some five-foot by ten-foot trench units contain precisely the vertical order of ceramic varieties that might be predicted. In others, the pattern is reversed with no available explanation for the discontinuity. The situation is further complicated since portions of the trenches cut through the flanks of Mound 2, thus creating considerable variation in the true elevation of the uppermost level of each excavation unit. In short, it is not entirely safe to equate similarly designated levels of successive horizontal proveniences along the entire spans of trenches ranging from seventy to 400 feet in length. Nevertheless, for the non-profiled trenches there is no alternative, and ceramic counts list level totals as if a given level falls within the same occupational stratum along the entire trench. Resulting interpretations must take into account the inherent methodological fallacy of such a procedure.

Considering the difficulties posed by the missing profiles, one cannot expect ideal stratigraphic results. Indeed, it is somewhat amazing that the overall results conform to predictions as well as they do. As demonstrated in the following analysis, the collections exhibit a comforting tendency for the early varieties, such as *Mabin* and *Crooks*, to be deepest and the Baptiste phase varieties to be towards the surface. The trend is strong enough to leave the impression that the 1939 excavations did uncover clear site stratigraphy, an impression which would be even stronger if complete profiles were available to leaven the analysis.

Trenches A, B, and D.—The three shallowest trenches, all devoid of cataloged ceramics below a depth of fifteen inches, are designated Trenches A, B, and D. As was shown in Figure 25, Trench A is located west of Mound 2 and, in terms of the site grid, runs from E100-105, S080-090 to E100-105, S370-380. To simplify analysis, the ten-foot sections of the trench by which material is cataloged are defined here as excavation units which go from unit 1 on the northern end to unit 27 on the southern end. Levels are uniformly three inches in depth. Similarly, Trench B is also on the western flank of Mound 2, specifically from E150-155, S060-070 to E150-155, S370-380. It is divided into excavation units beginning with unit 28 on the northern end and continuing to unit 102 on the southern end. A number of additional squares, ten feet on a side, were added onto the central portion of Trench B, and these are included in the numbering of Trench B excavation units. Finally, Trench D is east of Mound 2 from E500-505, S120-130 to E500-505, S370-380 and is divided from north to south into excavation units 143 to 168.

Although it was 300 feet long, Trench A yielded very few ceramics, all of which came from units 23, 25, and 26 on the southern end. It must be

TABLE 9

CERAMIC COUNTS, TRENCH A

	LEVELS				
	A/B	C	D	E	TOTAL
Marksville Incised					
var. Marksville	1	5			6
wide-spaced	(1)	(5)			
var. unspecified			2		2
Marksville Stamped					
var. Mabin			1	1	2
cord-wrapped stick			(1)	(1)	
Total	1	5	3	1	10

	LEVELS				
	A/B	C	D	E	TOTAL
Diagnostic Modes					
Marksville rims		1			1
vertical incised		(1)			
notched rims			1		1
Total	0	1	1	0	2

concluded that most of Trench A fell outside the locus of village occupation. Trench A ceramics, listed in Table 9, are too few to be at all conclusive. They seem to belong to the Marksville phase exclusively. Perhaps noteworthy is the fact that the only variety found in the deepest level, E, is *Mabin*. Levels A and B, measuring from the surface to six inches, constitute the plow zone and are merged in Table 9 and all subsequent tables.

Ceramics are only slightly more abundant in Trench B (Table 10). Most excavation units contain very few decorated sherds, and sterile levels are

TABLE 10

CERAMIC COUNTS, TRENCH B

	LEVELS							
	A/B	C	D	E	F	G	PIT	TOTAL
Marksville Incised								
var. Marksville	16	16	9	1			2	44
close-spaced	(3)	(6)	(4)				(1)	
wide-spaced	(13)	(10)	(3)	(1)				
line-filled			(2)				(1)	
var. Yokena	1			3				4
var. unspecified		1					1	2
Marksville Stamped								
var. Marksville	6	6	6	1		2	3	24
var. Crooks		1		2				3
var. Mabin	2		2					4
cord-wrapped	(2)		(2)					
var. Troyville	5	12	7	2				26
var. unspecified	3	4	1				1	9
Indian Bay Stamped								
var. unspecified	1							1
Unclassified	3							3
Total	37	40	25	9	0	2	7	120

	LEVELS							
	A/B	C	D	E	F	G	PIT	TOTAL
Diagnostic Modes								
Marksville rims	1	1	2				1	5
crosshatched			(2)					
vertical inc.		(1)					(1)	
slanted inc.	(1)							
notched rims	3		2					5
lines across lip	1							1
Total	5	1	4	0	0	0	1	11

present in many individual units. Except for four sherds of *Yokena*, three of which occur unpredictably in level E, the sample contains only Marksville phase varieties. *Troyville* is plentiful, as in the Setzler and Ford collections from the village area, and it surpasses the type variety of Marksville Stamped in frequency. The wide-spaced treatment of Marksville Incised, *var. Marksville* holds a two to one edge over the close-spaced treatment, and the line-filled triangle treatment is barely represented. In all, the Trench B ceramics do not illuminate Marksville stratigraphy to any great extent.

Units 80, 83, and 84 of Trench B, as well as a unit labeled "pit," coincide with the provenience of the poorly defined House B. The ceramic sample from these units amounts to only twenty-seven sherds, and the count includes all levels rather than a specific house floor deposit. In contrast to House A, the sample contains no Baptiste phase markers, but neither does it contain *Crooks, Mabin,* or other highly diagnostic early Marksville markers. *Troyville* and the type varieties of Marksville Stamped and Marksville Incised are approximately equally distributed. There is one vertically incised Marksville rim. Overall, the sample is not sufficient to clearly date House B. Superficially, and again in contrast to House A, the House B ceramic sample seems to indicate a Marksville phase identification.

Trench D is more complicated than Trenches A and B because there are more Baptiste phase markers, but it is just as unsatisfying from the standpoint of stratigraphy (Table 11). The yield of Trench D is fairly high, especially in the southern half, and fewer levels of individual units are sterile. As in the other trenches, ceramic density decreases with depth. Of the Baptiste phase varieties, all but *Manny* are confined to the upper levels. *Manny*, however, is found in levels C and D where it ought not occur. Also discomforting is the fact that *Mabin* is found in all levels with a maximum density in level C. There is no *Crooks*, and only a very little *Troyville* which shows up in the upper levels. The sample contains a large number of Marksville rims, again most plentiful in the plow zone. Without profiles, there is no way to reconcile the lack of separation between varieties of the Marksville and Baptiste phases. Until such time as the profiles can be located, Table 11 preserves a record of variety distribution by level without contributing measurably to the solution of Marksville chronology.

Trench C.—The longest trench, and also the one which cuts most deeply through the edge of Mound 2, is located between E100-110, S380-385 and E490-500, S380-385. Trench C includes excavation units here numbered 104 to 142 from west to east. Unlike the situation for the previous trenches, there is a small-scale profile for the central portion of Trench C. Vescelius (1957: Fig. 1) illustrates "profile A" which includes excavation units 119 through 135. By photographically enlarging the Vescelius profile to a workable scale, and then superimposing the vertical and horizontal provenience contained in the catalog record, it has been possible to tie the collections, at least approximately, to actual site strata. The profile of the central section of Trench C is redrawn as Figure 31.

The two upper layers of Trench C, stratum IA and stratum IB, are described as "recent topsoil" (Vescelius, 1957:418), and might logically

TABLE 11

CERAMIC COUNTS, TRENCH D

	LEVELS				
	A/B	C	D	E	TOTAL
Marksville Incised					
var. Marksville	22	15	11	2	50
close-spaced	(6)	(6)	(4)		
wide-spaced	(10)	(7)	(6)	(1)	
line-filled	(6)	(2)	(1)	(1)	
var. Yokena	1				1
var. Leist		1			1
var. unspecified	4	4	2	1	11
Marksville Stamped					
var. Marksville	45	34	13	4	96
var. Mabin	2	9	3	1	15
cord-wrapped stick	(1)	(7)	(2)	(1)	
straight dentate	(1)	(2)	(1)		
var. Troyville	4	1			5
var. Manny		2	3		5
var. Newsome	1				1
var. unspecified	5	3	3	2	13
Catahoula Zoned Red					
var. Catahoula			1		1
Indian Bay Stamped					
var. unspecified	1				1
Churupa Punctated					
var. unspecified			1	1	2
Unclassified	2		1		3
Total	87	69	38	11	205

	A/B	C	D	E	TOTAL
Diagnostic Modes					
Marksville rims	15	9	3	1	28
crosshatched	(7)	(5)	(2)		
vertical incised	(1)	(2)			
slanted incised	(4)	(1)		(1)	
alt. slanted	(3)	(1)	(1)		
notched rims		1			1
lines across lip		3	2		5
Total	15	13	5	1	34

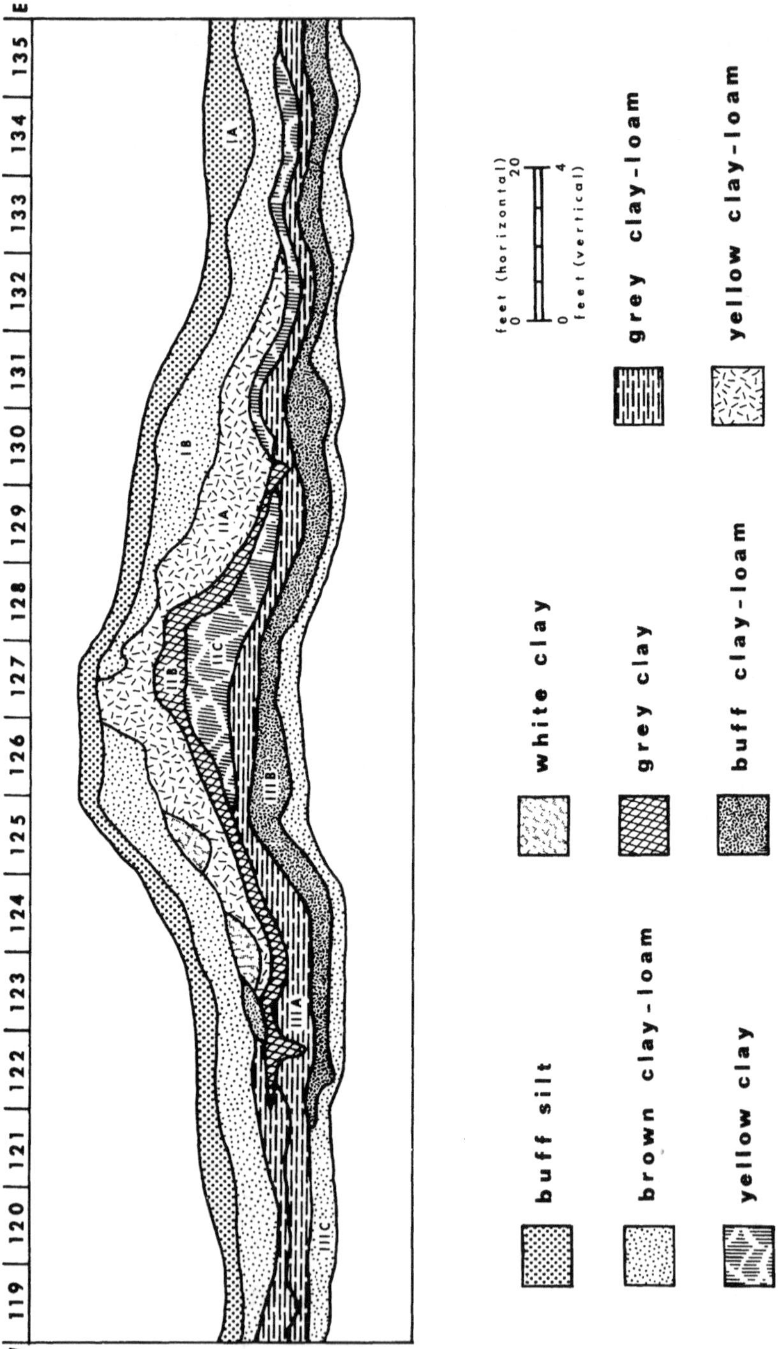

Fig. 31. Trench C Profile

represent slope-wash, especially in view of Fowke's statements on the instability of Mound 2 construction materials (Fowke, 1928:414). Strata IA and IB consist of buff silt and brown clay-loam respectively. The next three strata, designated IIA, IIB, and IIC, are equated with separate mantles of Mound 2, stratum IIC representing the earliest construction stage (Vescelius, 1957:418). Finally, strata IIIA, IIIB, and IIIC are described as "subsoil" (Vescelius, 1957:418).

A re-examination of the Trench C profile leads to a conclusion on the structure of Mound 2 which coincides with Vescelius' analysis with one exception: strata IA and IB, and their contents, appear to have accumulated in place during the final periods of mound–or site–utilization. They are not indicative of recent deposition, or slope-wash, for several reasons. First, the brown clay-loam of stratum IB originates in the layer of the same material that underlies the entire site (see Figure 31, stratum IIIC). Since it is found not above stratum IB but rather beneath Mound 2, the brown clay-loam must have been purposefully deposited, possibly during a fourth stage of mound construction. Further, the ceramic contents of strata IA and IB point to a probable temporal division between the two upper layers. It is the ceramic discontinuity that affords the greatest potential for deciphering the chronology of Mound 2, and hence the ceramic distribution needs to be put into proper perspective.

Table 12 lists the ceramic counts for the several strata that are found in the section of Trench C that is profiled. As can be seen, all but five of the sherds fall into one of the two upper strata. Ceramics of the Marksville and Baptiste phases are mixed in the upper layer of buff silt, but stratum IB appears to comprise a pure level of Marksville phase ceramics which caps all of the mound beneath it. The only incidence of *Crooks* is in stratum IB, and the other early diagnostic, *Mabin*, is fairly plentiful in the same layer of brown clay-loam. Beneath stratum IB, there is precious little material, but what there is seems to date early Marksville. Particularly noteworthy is the fact that the two deepest sherds, both in level N of unit 126, are good examples of the cord-wrapped stick treatment of variety *Mabin*. Unfortunately, the deep material in strata IIA, IIB, and IIC cannot be assigned to specific mantles of Mound 2 because levels of the long ten-foot excavation units overlap more than one stratum of the sloping mound deposits. All that can be said with confidence is that early Marksville sherds are included in the fill of the second, and possibly the first, construction stage of Mound 2.

The ceramic contents of the non-profiled sections of Trench C are listed by level in Table 13, the result being a reflection of the situation encountered in the other trenches. The Baptiste varieties, *Yokena* and *Newsome*, are found in the upper levels, and the early Marksville diagnostics attain higher percentages of the level totals in direct proportion to depth. The frequency of *Mabin* and the Marksville rims in the lower levels is especially encouraging. In

TABLE 12

CERAMIC COUNTS, PROFILED SECTION OF TRENCH C

	STRATA					
	IA	IB	IIA	IIB	IIC	TOTAL
Marksville Incised						
var. Marksville	18	22	? ←1→ ?			41
close-spaced	(10)	(6)				
wide-spaced	(5)	(13)		(1)		
line-filled	(3)	(3)				
var. Yokena	6					6
var. unspecified	1	3				4
Marksville Stamped						
var. Marksville	11	13				24
var. Crooks		1				1
var. Mabin	2	5		? ←2→ ?		9
cord-wrapped	(2)	(3)		(2)		
straight dent.		(2)				
var. Troyville	1	3				4
var. Manny	1					1
var. unspecified	6	6				12
Indian Bay Stamped						
var. Cypress Bayou	1					1
var. unspecified			1			1
Unclassified	1	1				2
Total	48	54	1	1	2	106

	STRATA					
	IA	IB	IIA	IIB	IIC	TOTAL
Diagnostic Modes						
Marksville rims	5	3				8
crosshatched	(4)	(1)				
vertical inc.	(1)					
slanted inc.		(1)				
plain band,		(1)				
Notched rims	1		? ←1→ ?			2
Two-Line cir.	1					1
Total	7	3		1		11

fact, the apparent separation of early and late Marksville material is so convincing that one is tempted to speculate that the two upper strata shown in Figure 31 continue into the village area both east and west of the section of Trench C that is profiled. If so, Table 13 suggests that the dividing line between them falls within level C, the lower stratum (IB) representing a

Marksville phase occupation, and the upper stratum (IA) a mixture of debris from the Marksville and Baptiste phases.

Trench E.—The shortest trench, but one of the potentially most valuable cuts for unraveling site stratigraphy is located northeast of Mound 2 from S055-060, E540-550 to S055-060, E600-610. From west to east, Trench E includes units 169 through 175. As recently pointed out by Neitzel (November 1973, personal communication), Trench E cuts across the rim of the Marksville Prairie and includes a portion of the slope descending to Old River:

TABLE 13

CERAMIC COUNTS, NON-PROFILED SECTIONS OF TRENCH C

	LEVELS						
	A/B	C	D	E	F	G	TOTAL
Marksville Incised							
var. Marksville	6	14	11	13	5	2	51
close-spaced	(3)	(5)	(3)	(8)	(1)	(1)	
wide-spaced	(2)	(7)	(6)	(3)	(3)		
line-filled	(1)	(2)	(2)	(2)	(1)	(1)	
var. Yokena	1	1					2
var. unspecified		1	2	1	1		5
Marksville Stamped							
var. Marksville	7	9	7	5	2	2	32
var. Crooks		1					1
var. Mabin	1	2	5		1	1	10
cord-wrapped	(1)	(2)	(5)				
straight dent.					(1)	(1)	
var. Troyville		2					2
var. Newsome	1						1
var. unspecified	2	2	1	6			11
Unclassified			1	1			2
Total	18	32	27	26	9	5	117

	LEVELS						
	A/B	C	D	E	F	G	TOTAL
Diagnostic Modes							
Marksville rims		1		2	1		4
crosshatched		(1)					
vertical inc.				(2)			
plain band					(1)		
lines across lip		1					1
Total	0	2	0	2	1	0	5

> There should be a profile for the over-the-edge strata cut on the extreme edge of the bluff east of Mound 2. It was simple midden, perhaps 1.5 feet thick, arching over the bluff edge.

The profile referred to by Neitzel is illustrated by Vescelius (1957: Fig. 1) as "profile B" and includes the entirety of Trench E. Again, by photographically enlarging the Vescelius illustration and superimposing the provenience data, the ceramics from Trench E can be analyzed in terms of actual site strata. The profile of Trench E is redrawn as Figure 32.

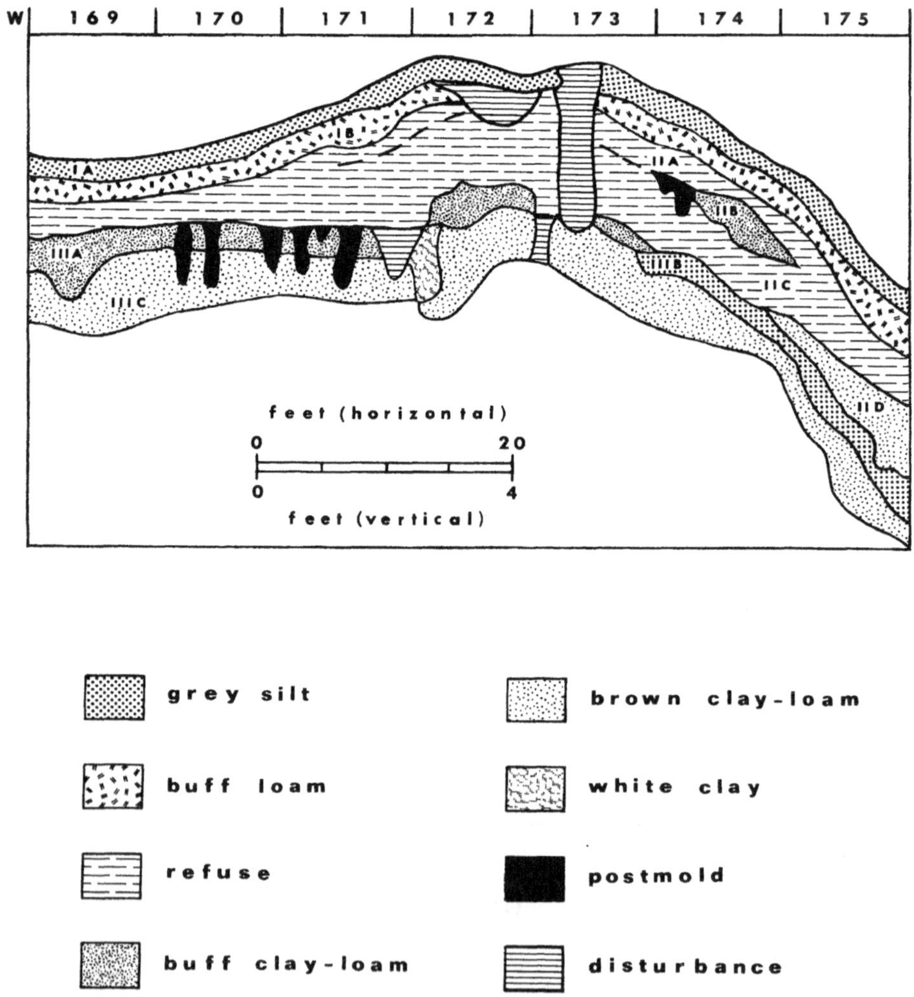

Fig. 32. Trench E Profile

Unfortunately, efforts to tie Trench E ceramics to site stratigraphy are less successful than in the case of the Trench C profile. The reason for the lack of success is, of course, the length of the excavation units which measure five by ten feet. Levels of individual units overlap several of the sloping strata, thus denying positive association of ceramics to stratum. The situation is especially aggravated in the eastern half of the trench where the slope of the bluff is encountered. As a result, the ceramic counts in Table 14 are listed by level rather than by the more meaningful association, stratum.

At first glance, Table 14 appears to negate previous efforts to define Marksville chronology, or at least to reflect mixed stratigraphy. The major difficulties, however, can be resolved with the aid of the existing profile. All of the Baptiste phase material, namely varieties *Yokena, Manny,* and *Newsome*, is from excavation units 172 and 173. As can be seen in Figure 32, both of these units contain major disturbances which can easily account for the scrambled ceramic associations. Deleting the two disturbed units, the ceramic distribution of Trench E is similar to the results from Trench C. As expected, the deepest levels—G and below—contain both *Crooks* and *Mabin*. In this case, the early Marksville diagnostics are joined by *Cypress Bayou* which may also be an early marker, although its frequency is too low everywhere at the site to be conclusive.

Examination of the Trench E ceramic counts provided by Vescelius (1957: Table 3) reaffirms the fact that the present analysis may not be dealing with the entire 1939 collection. Vescelius includes minority representations of Beldeau Incised, Mulberry Creek Cord Marked, and Marksville Red Filmed in the Trench E counts. None of these very recognizable decorations could be found in the present sample. Fortunately, Vescelius records their presence in levels C and D, both apparently mixed levels, rather than in the lower levels where all but Marksville Red Filmed—renamed Catahoula Zoned Red by Phillips (1970:63)—would be incongruous in an early Marksville context.

It should be noted, finally, that the midden encountered in Trench E consists of two parts, separated in places by a lens of mottled buff clay-loam (Vescelius, 1957:418). The upper portion (stratum IIA) is grayish black soil and the lower portion (stratum IIC) dark brown. The division confirms, possibly, the presence of two phases of site occupation which were postulated through ceramic analysis in the other trenches. In short, although inconclusive, Trench E ceramics are compatible with the thesis that the Marksville site stratigraphy surrounding Mound 2 consists of an early Marksville phase midden overlain by a layer of mixed Marksville and Baptiste phase debris.

Summary.—The 1939 trenches provide the best chronological information pertaining to the sequence of occupation at Marksville, and they begin to date Mound 2 construction. When the percentage of level totals is computed for the key Marksville varieties and that percentage is plotted

TABLE 14.

CERAMIC COUNTS, TRENCH E

	LEVELS							
	A/B	C	D	E	F	G	>G	TOTAL
Marksville Incised								
var. Marksville	9	6	2	3	7	3	2	32
close-spaced	(1)	(1)	(2)	(1)			(1)	
wide-spaced	(7)	(3)		(1)	(5)	(3)	(1)	
line-filled	(1)	(2)		(1)	(2)			
var. Yokena					1			1
var. unspecified					1			1
Marksville Stamped								
var. Marksville	19	24	15	12	11	7	1	89
var. Crooks		1		1		1		3
var. Mabin		1	1		1		1	4
cord-wrapped		(1)	(1)		(1)			
straight dent.							(1)	
var. Troyville	1	1	1	1	1			5
var. Manny			1	1				2
var. Newsome				4	3			7
var. unspecified	2	1	1			1		5
Indian Bay Stamped								
var. Cypress Bayou					1	1		2
var. unspecified	1							1
Total	32	34	21	22	26	13	4	152

	LEVELS							
	A/B	C	D	E	F	G	>G	TOTAL
Diagnostic Modes								
Marksville rims	7	4	4	4	6			25
crosshatched	(4)		(1)	(4)	(4)			
vertical inc.		(1)			(1)			
slanted inc.	(1)	(2)			(1)			
alt. slanted	(2)		(2)					
dash-dot		(1)						
plain band			(1)					
notched rims					1			1
Total	7	4	4	4	7	0	0	26

against depth (Fig. 33), a ceramic distribution can be seen in the trenches which suggests a clear shift in prevailing Marksville varieties. Figure 33 is based on all excavation units except the pit in Trench B and units 172 and 173 of

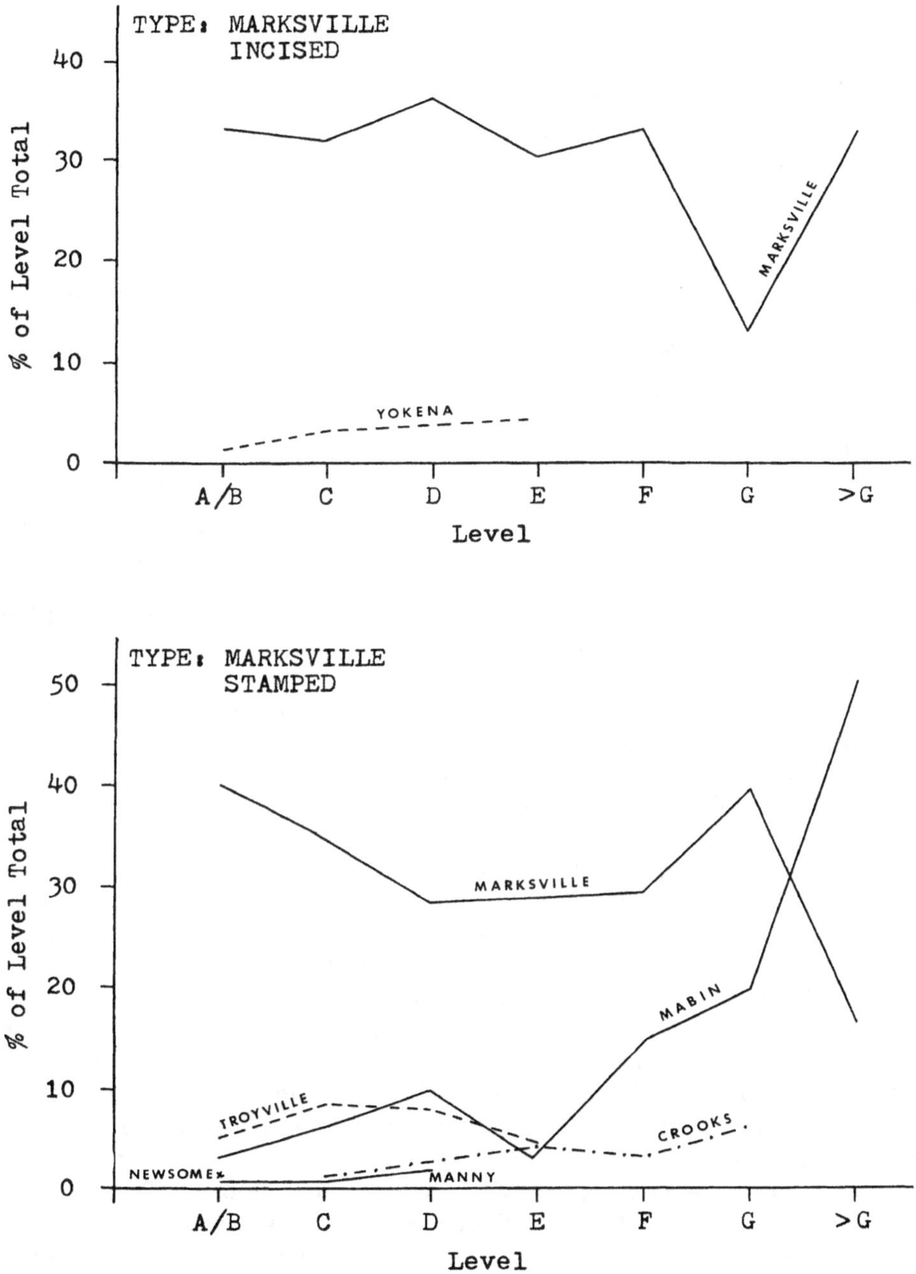

Fig. 33. Variety distribution by level

Trench E which are known to be disturbed. The clearest trend is revealed by the Marksville Stamped varieties. Below level E, variety *Marksville* decreases in frequency while *Mabin* and *Crooks* each achieve significant gains in their percentages of level totals. Considering the uncertainties inherent in the sample, the ceramic distribution in the trenches accords extremely well with the Marksville ceramic sequence developed for other sites in the Lower Mississippi Valley (Toth, 1972).

Although relating solely to the village area surrounding Mound 2, the evidence from the trenches—especially Trench C—suggests that the first use of this portion of the site was during the classic Marksville phase. *Crooks, Mabin,* and the Marksville rims are the best diagnostics of early Marksville, but the type varieties of Marksville Stamped and Marksville Incised—and possibly *Troyville* and *Cypress Bayou*—are part of the assemblage from the beginning. The separation between the first Marksville occupation and the succeeding Baptiste phase is indistinct, but apparently the shift is marked by the demise of *Crooks* and *Mabin*, the appearance of *Yokena, Leist, Manny, Newsome*, and other late varieties, and an improvement in the paste characteristics of ceramic manufacture. Presumably, the Marksville rims also disappeared prior to the Baptiste phase, and the better paste was added to the *Marksville* varieties of Marksville Stamped and Marksville Incised—and to *Troyville*—thus yielding the Baptiste phase varieties shown in the ceramic counts. The final Baptiste occupation, or use, of the Marksville site seems short-lived, possibly because the resident population found it advantageous to move to another location on the edge of the Marksville Prairie, namely the Baptiste site which is about two miles to the south.

The preceding reconstruction of the occupational sequence at Marksville is admittedly built on very slim evidence. The collections do seem to reflect, however, a continuum of ceramic wares and decorations that is compatible with the reconstruction. One gets the distinct impression that a single population is involved, and that after the initial introduction of Hopewellian ceramics the development is local and continuous. Such a hypothesis can be tested only by further excavation at the Marksville site.

As to the dating of Mound 2, the ceramics from the profiled section of Trench C seem to indicate that the major stages of mound construction were carried out during the Marksville phase. Nonetheless, there are so few sherds from within the mound (strata IIA, IIB, and IIC) that the possibility of an earlier association cannot be ruled out. Heretical or not, it would be unwise to discard prematurely the alternative hypothesis that the major portion of Mound 2 was erected during the Tchefuncte or, more probably, Poverty Point period. The handful of Marksville phase sherds found within the mound might be intrusive, the result of some undetected disturbance. Whatever the earliest date of mound construction, which at present seems to be during the Marksville phase, there is nothing to indicate that Mound 2 was completed—or even used—later than the Baptiste phase.

CONCLUSION

THE foregoing discussions on the history of Marksville archaeology and the ceramics derived from past excavations highlight a number of unanswered questions pertaining to the cultural dynamics involved at one of the most important sites in the Lower Mississippi Valley. It should be obvious that these far-reaching problems can be solved only by more archaeology, problem-oriented archaeology that is designed to test specific hypotheses. Marksville must be revisited. By way of overall summary, then, a survey of the research objectives suggested by the conclusions of this paper is offered with the hope that it will provide a measure of direction to future Marksville archaeology.

The Marksville ceramic collections indicate the presence of three components at the site, and there is the possibility of a fourth, non-ceramic, component in the neighborhood. The relationship between the Marksville and Baptiste components is fairly clear, and a population shift to the Baptiste site during the final phases of site utilization has been postulated. The circumstances surrounding the relationship between Marksville and an earlier Tchefuncte component are far less certain. Although there is a trace of Tchefuncte decorated pottery at the site, and a very real continuity exists between the ceramic wares of the Tchefuncte and the Marksville phases, the Tchefuncte component at Marksville is of insufficient depth to illuminate the transition between the phases. Thus, one important research objective is to survey the Marksville Prairie and the surrounding floodplain for Tchefuncte components of larger magnitude. The Moncla site in northern Avoyelles Parish, a site greatly destroyed by Red River levee construction, comes to mind as an example of the kind of site at which to examine the Tchefuncte to Marksville transition. Other such sites can, it is hoped, be located.

In similar fashion, Poverty Point activity on the Marksville Prairie needs to be scrutinized more closely. Components are known to be present at Marksville—especially in Mound 10—and at the Three Prong Lake site on the western margin of the prairie. More thorough survey work will no doubt disclose additional locations. It is important to define a Poverty Point phase for the Marksville Prairie and surrounding environs because it is entirely possible that such a phase begins a cultural continuum that evolves directly, though modified by outside influence, into that manifestation found at Marksville. In this respect, it is imperative to test the hypothesis that some of the undated site features at Marksville—the earthworks, Mounds 2 and 6—may belong to an earlier phase. The well-preserved section of the embankment at the southern end of the site offers the best chance of dating the earthworks. Cross-sectioning it and analyzing its contents should be the first priority. Similarly, Mounds 2 and 6 must be opened to expose their internal structure and to date their construction once and for all. The mounds present a formidable enterprise, but the work can be aided by the careful employment of earth moving equipment.

Marksville subsistence and settlement represent areas of cultural activity that are, at present, totally unexplored. That situation must change if Marksville is to be fairly compared with other contemporaneous cultural systems for which subsistence settlement data are increasingly available. At the outset, the circular features outside the main enclosure, so clearly delimited on aerial photographs, must be investigated while a few are still intact or the hypothesis that they represent the dwelling sites of a resident Marksville population can never be tested. Undisturbed portions of the midden within the enclosure require further testing as well, this time by excavation designed to recover subsistence data through screening, flotation, and similar techniques. Such excavations may also provide materials for radiocarbon dating, the requirement for which hardly needs to be emphasized in connection with the Marksville phase. Certain knowledge of what a Marksville house looks like is yet another pressing research objective.

In short, an exciting period of Marksville archaeology still lies ahead. I am convinced that continued refinement of the ceramic sequence, through use of the type-variety system, holds the key to the successful attainment of future research objectives. Tightly defined ceramic varieties and modes will lead to equally well-defined Marksville phases throughout the Lower Mississippi Valley. Only then will there be the synchronic perspective necessary to effectively integrate new information on subsistence, settlement, trade, intra- and inter-regional interaction, and other components of the Marksville cultural system. If this paper contributes in any way towards that stable base for future Marksville archaeology, the time and effort that went into it were well spent.

BIBLIOGRAPHY

Beyer, George E.

1900 Mound Investigations at Lemar, Louisiana. Publications of the Louisiana Historical Society, Vol. 2, Pt. 3, for 1899-1900, pp. 28-33. New Orleans.

Binford, Lewis R.

1964 A Consideration of Archaeological Research Design. American Antiquity 29:425-444.

Bohannon, Charles F.

1972 Excavations at the Pharr Mounds, Prentiss and Itawamba Counties Mississippi. Publication of the U.S. Department of the Interior, National Park Service, Office of Archeology and Historic Preservation, Division of Archeology and Anthropology. Washington, D.C.

Brain, J. P., Alan Toth and A. Rodriguez-Buckingham

1974 Ethnohistoric Archaeology and the De Soto Entrada into the Lower Mississippi Valley. The Conference on Historic Site Archaeology Papers, Vol. 7:232-289.

Brown, Clair A.

1944 Historical Commentary on the Distribution of Vegetation in Louisiana and Some Recent Observations. Proceedings of the Louisiana Academy of Sciences, Vol. 8:35-47.

1945 Louisiana Trees and Shrubs. Louisiana Forestry Commission Bulletin No. 1. New Orleans.

Chawner, William D.

1936 Geology of Catahoula and Concordia Parishes. Department of Conservation, Louisiana Geological Survey, Geological Bulletin No. 9. New Orleans.

Fisk, Harold N.

1940 Geology of Avoyelles and Rapides Parishes. Department of Conservation, Louisiana Geological Survey, Geological Bulletin No. 18. New Orleans.

1944 Geological Investigation of the Alluvial Valley of the Lower Mississippi River. War Department, Corps of Engineers, U.S. Army, Mississippi River Commission Publication No. 52. Vicksburg.

Flannery, Kent V.
1973 Archeology with a Capital "S." *In* Research and Theory in Current Archeology, C. L. Redman, ed., John Wiley & Sons. New York.

Ford, James A.
1934 Mound Builders Were Pit Dwellers. El Palacio 36:74-75.
1936 Analysis of Indian Village Site Collections from Louisiana and Mississippi. Department of Conservation, Louisiana Geological Survey, Anthropological Study No. 2. New Orleans.
1939 Archaeological Exploration in Louisiana During 1938. Louisiana Conservation Review, Vol. 7, No. 4:15-17. New Orleans.
1951 Greenhouse: A Troyville-Coles Creek Period Site in Avoyelles Parish, Louisiana. Anthropological Papers of the American Museum of Natural History, Vol. 44, Pt. 1. New York.
1969 A Comparison of Formative Cultures in the Americas: Diffusion or the Psychic Unity of Man? Smithsonian Institution Contributions to Anthropology, Vol. 11. Washington.

Ford, James A. and George I. Quimby, Jr.
1945 The Tchefuncte Culture, An Early Occupation of the Lower Mississippi Valley. Memoirs of the Society for American Archaeology, No. 2. Menasha, Wisconsin.

Ford, James A. and Clarence H. Webb
1956 Poverty Point, A Late Archaic Site in Louisiana. Anthropological Papers of the American Museum of Natural History, Vol. 46, Pt. 1. New York.

Ford, James A. and Gordon Willey
1940 Crooks Site, a Marksville Period Burial Mound in La Salle Parish, Louisiana. Department of Conservation, Louisiana Geological Survey, Anthropological Study No. 3. New Orleans.

Fowke, Gerard
1927 Archeological Work in Louisiana. Smithsonian Miscellaneous Collections, Vol. 78, No. 7:254-259. Washington.
1928 Archeological Investigations - II: Explorations in the Red River Valley in Louisiana. Forty-fourth Annual Report of the Bureau of American Ethnology, pp. 399-436; plates 64-69. Washington.

Freeman, Thomas and Peter Custis
1806 An Account of the Red River in Louisiana, drawn up from the returns of Messrs. Freeman & Custis to the War Office of the United States, who explored the same in the year 1806. Washington, D.C.

Greengo, Robert E.
1964 Issaquena: An Archaeological Phase in the Yazoo Basin of the Lower Mississippi Valley. Memoirs of the Society for American Archaeology, No. 18. Salt Lake City.

Griffin, James B.
1973 Review of Philip Phillips, 1970, *In* American Antiquity 38:374-380.

Haas, Mary R.
1950 Tunica Texts. University Publications in Linguistics, Vol. 6, No. 1:1-74. University of California Press, Berkeley.

Hayes, Ralph W.
1945 Trees and Forests of Louisiana. Louisiana State University Press, Baton Rouge.

Moore, Clarence B.
1908 Certain Mounds of Arkansas and Mississippi–Part II: Mounds of the Lower Yazoo and Lower Sunflower Rivers, Mississippi. Journal of the Academy of Natural Sciences of Philadelphia, 13: 564-592. Philadelphia.
1912 Some Aboriginal Sites on the Red River. Journal of the Academy of Natural Sciences of Philadelphia, 14:482-644. Philadelphia.

O'Pry, Maude Hearn
1928 Chronicles of Shreveport. Journal Printing Co., Shreveport.

Perino, Gregory H.
1968 The Pete Klunk Mound Group, Calhoun County, Illinois: The Archaic and Hopewell Occupations (With an Appendix on the Gibson Mound Group). *In* "Hopewellian and Woodland Site Archaeology in Illinois," J. A. Brown, ed. Illinois Archaeological Survey Bulletin No. 6. Urbana.

Phillips, Philip
1970 Archaeological Survey in the Lower Yazoo Basin, Mississippi, 1949-1955. Papers of the Peabody Museum of Archaeology and Ethnology, Harvard University, Vol. 60, Parts 1 and 2. Cambridge.

Phillips, Philip, James A. Ford and James B. Griffin
1951 Archaeological Survey in the Lower Mississippi Alluvial Valley 1940-1947. Papers of the Peabody Museum of Archaeology and Ethnology, Harvard University, Vol. 25. Cambridge.

Prufer, Olaf H.
1964 The Hopewell Complex of Ohio. *In* "Hopewellian Studies," J. R. Caldwell and R. L. Hall, eds. Illinois State Museum Scientific Papers, Vol. 12.

Redman, Charles L.
1973 Research and Theory in Current Archeology: An Introduction. *In* Research and Theory in Current Archeology, C. L. Redman, ed. John Wiley and Sons. New York.

Rouse, Irving
1972 Introduction to Prehistory: A Systematic Approach. McGraw-Hill. New York.
1973 Analytic, Synthetic, and Comparative Archeology. *In* Research and Theory in Current Archeology, C. L. Redman, ed. John Wiley & Sons. New York.

Saucier, Corinne L.
1943 History of Avoyelles Parish, Louisiana. Pelican Publishing Company. New Orleans.

Saucier, Roger T.

1971 Quaternary Geology of the Lower Mississippi Valley. Unpublished manuscript sponsored by the Arkansas Archeological Survey and prepared by the U.S. Army Engineer Waterways Experiment Station. Vicksburg.

Sears, William H.

1964 The Southeastern United States. *In* Prehistoric Man in the New World, J. D. Jennings and E. Norbeck, eds. University of Chicago Press. Chicago.

Setzler, Frank M.

1933*a* Hopewell Type Pottery from Louisiana. Journal of the Washington Academy of Sciences, Vol. 23, No. 3:149-153. Menasha, Wisconsin.

1933*b* Pottery of the Hopewell Type from Louisiana. Proceedings of the United States National Museum, Vol. 82, Art. 22:1-21; plates 1-7. Washington, D.C.

1934 A Phase of Hopewell Mound Builders in Louisiana. Explorations and Fieldwork of the Smithsonian Institution in 1933, pp. 38-40. Washington, D.C.

1940 Archeological Perspectives in the Northern Mississippi Valley. *In* "Essays in Historical Anthropology of North America," published in honor of John R. Swanton. Smithsonian Miscellaneous Collections, Vol. 100. Washington, D.C.

1943 Archaeological Explorations in the United States, 1930-1942. Acta Americana, Vol. 1, No. 2:206-220.

n.d. Marksville: A Louisiana Variant of the Hopewell Culture. Manuscript in preparation.

Setzler, Frank M. and William Duncan Strong

1936 Archaeology and Relief. American Antiquity 1:301-309.

Skipwith, H.

1881 Avoyelles Parish. *In* Louisiana: Products, Resources and Attractions; with a sketch of the parishes, William H. Harris, ed. New Orleans Democrat Print, New Orleans.

Struever, Stuart

1971 Comments on Archaeological Data Requirements and Research Strategy. American Antiquity 36:9-19.

Struever, Stuart and Kent D. Vickery

1973 The Beginnings of Cultivation in the Midwest-Riverine Area of the United States. American Anthropologist 75:1197-1220.

Swanton, John R.

1911 Indian Tribes of the Lower Mississippi Valley and Adjacent Coast of the Gulf of Mexico. Bureau of American Ethnology, Bulletin 43. Washington, D.C.

Taylor, Walter W.

1948 A Study of Archeology. Memoirs of the American Anthropological Association, No. 69. Menasha.

1972 Old Wine and New Skins: A Contemporary Parable. *In* Contemporary Archaeology, M. P. Leone, ed. Southern Illinois University Press. Carbondale and Edwardsville, Ill.

Toth, Alan

1966 Hopewellian Influence in the Southeastern United States. Unpublished honors thesis, Department of Anthropology, Harvard University.

1972 The Marksville Period in the Lower Mississippi Valley. Paper read at the 37th annual meeting of the Society for American Archaeology. Miami, Florida.

1973 Statistical Analysis of Marksville Ceramics. Unpublished manuscript, Department of Anthropology, Harvard University.

Vescelius, Gary S.

1957 Mound 2 at Marksville. American Antiquity 22:416-420.

Walker, Winslow

1932 A Reconnaissance of Northern Louisiana Mounds. Explorations and Fieldwork of the Smithsonian Institution in 1931, pp. 169-174. Washington, D.C.

1936 The Troyville Mounds, Catahoula Parish, Louisiana. Bureau of American Ethnology, Bulletin 113. Washington, D.C.

Willey, Gordon R.

1966 An Introduction to American Archaeology, Vol. 1: North and Middle America. Prentice-Hall. Englewood Cliffs, N.J.

Williamson, George

1883 Abstracts from Anthropological Correspondence. Annual Report of the Smithsonian Institution for the Year 1881, pp. 681-686. Washington, D.C.

APPENDIX

ROSTER OF TYPES AND VARIETIES PRESENT AT MARKSVILLE

ALTHOUGH the purpose of providing an appendix on the ceramic types and varieties present at Marksville is twofold, it is not the intent here to rewrite the excellent descriptions already provided by Phillips (1970). Rather, the following pages endeavor to complement the Marksville type and variety definitions offered by Phillips, who, it must be noted, did not have the advantage of access to large collections from sites that can be assigned to the Marksville phase. A second objective is to provide illustrative material that will facilitate an understanding of the discussions contained in the main body of this paper.

Since it would be repetitive in most cases to follow Phillips's format for type and variety descriptions exactly, a modified version is adopted herein. The ceramic write-ups, therefore, will be limited to the following headings: sorting criteria, distribution, and chronological position. For additional information on the background of and documentation for the various types and varieties considered, readers are referred to Phillips (1970). The procedure will be abbreviated still more for varieties, especially those of the Baptiste phase, which are found at Marksville in extremely small quantities and thus do not supply sufficient information to expand on the original definitions. All material illustrated in Figures 34 to 47 is from the Marksville site. Specific provenience information is listed at the bottom of each plate.

Baytown Plain, *var. Marksville*

The plain ware of the Marksville phase has a characteristic soft, chalky appearance which is also found on associated decorated ceramics. It intergrades between the preceding Tchefuncte Plain, *var. Tchefuncte* and the Baytown Plain, *var. Satartia* of the Baptiste phase.

Sorting criteria

The Marksville variety of Baytown Plain is distinguished by a soft, poorly fired paste that is tempered, perhaps unconsciously, with medium to large particles of what may be either pulverized potsherds or lumps of unprepared clay. The apparent deficiency in sifting procedures may also account for the occasional grit that is mixed with the clay tempering. Except for one vessel from Crooks (Ford and Willey, 1940: Fig. 32*b*), there is no reason to describe *Marksville* paste as "sandy." The surface of sherds, often heavily pitted as the result of leaching, is normally quite chalky and imparts a dusting of clay to the hands when handled. Despite the soft paste, some sherds exhibit a low polish in places. The average thickness is 6 to 7 mm, but at times it can range to nearly 1 cm.

Vessel modes associated with the *Marksville* variety include tubby pots, small beakers, straight jars with slight neck constrictions, and hemispherical bowls. Bases are predominantly flat and circular. The crosshatched Marksville rim is known to be associated with plain vessels (Ford and Willey, 1940: Fig. 22*d*), but there is no indication that the combination is common.

Distribution

A soft *Marksville* paste is found at all sites of the Marksville phase which, as presently defined, extend from the McDuffy site (16 Ct 15) in Catahoula Parish to the Medora site (16 WBR 1) west of Baton Rouge. It is characteristic of collections from both the Marksville and Crooks sites. The variety can be extended to the Point Lake phase in the Tensas Basin and to the Natchez Bluff district. Further investigation may reveal that it applies to all early Marksville phases in the Lower Mississippi Valley.

Chronological position

Bayton Plain, *var. Marksville* is firmly identified with the Marksville phase which is presumed to date somewhere within the time frame of 100 B.C. to A.D. 200. Further association with the Point Lake phase confirms that it is a marker for the early Marksville period. The ware was prevalent in much of the Lower Mississippi Valley at the time Hopewellian ceramic treatments and motifs were introduced.

Marksville Incised, *var. Marksville*
(Figures 34-36)

Highly diagnostic of the Marksville phase, the type variety of Marksville

Incised is found on ware similar to that described as Baytown Plain, *var. Marksville*. Sherds average 7 mm in thickness, but they tend to be slightly thinner than the equivalent variety of Marksville Stamped and are apt to have a harder, better polished surface. The variety is used with a number of decorative motifs, some of which are likely of Hopewellian inspiration, and vessel modes typical of the Marksville phase.

Sorting criteria

The incised lines of the *Marksville* variety are deep, wide, and U-shaped. They are applied to a surface that is leather-hard and smoothed or slightly polished, the result being fairly clean lines with minimal burr. Three distinct treatments, each associated with specific motifs, are included in the type variety. With better control, it may be possible at a future date to elevate some or all of the treatments to variety status.

Close-spaced treatment.—The most popular treatment of Marksville Incised, *var. Marksville* is characterized by parallel incised lines that are arranged in tight curvilinear or rectilinear patterns (Fig. 34). The concentric patterns include loops, triangles, circles, and squares. In each case, the width of the incised lines is about the same as the width of the space between lines. If the treatments described here are ever used to define new varieties, the close-spaced treatment should remain the type variety. It is the one most often found on mortuary vessels, and the treatment which best characterizes the ceramic collections from the Marksville and Crooks sites.

Wide-spaced treatment.—A decorative effect quite different from the close-spaced treatment is achieved by using similar incised lines in more open designs (Fig. 35). The emphasis is not on the contrast between alternating plain background and incised line, but rather on the design which is being outlined. The widely separated lines describe the bird motif, loose scrolls, open meandering designs, and simple patterns of parallel lines. In many respects, the wide-spaced treatment resembles the use of incised lines in varieties of Marksville Stamped except that the background is not roughened. The wide-spaced treatment, like the close-spaced treatment, is associated with the crosshatched and other Marksville rims.

Line-filled triangle treatment.—Wide, parallel incised lines are often applied to the rim zone of Marksville vessels, most often in a line-filled triangle arrangement (Fig. 36). The decoration is also found on the upper body of a vessel below a plain rim band. The widely spaced slanted lines may fill a distinct band that is zoned by incised lines that are parallel to the lip of the vessel, or they may be unzoned. At times, a row of hemiconical punctates lies below the band of decoration, thus suggesting strong affinity to the fine-line Marksville rim treatments. In fact, it might be reasonable to consider the line-filled triangle treatment as one variation of the Marksville rim. There

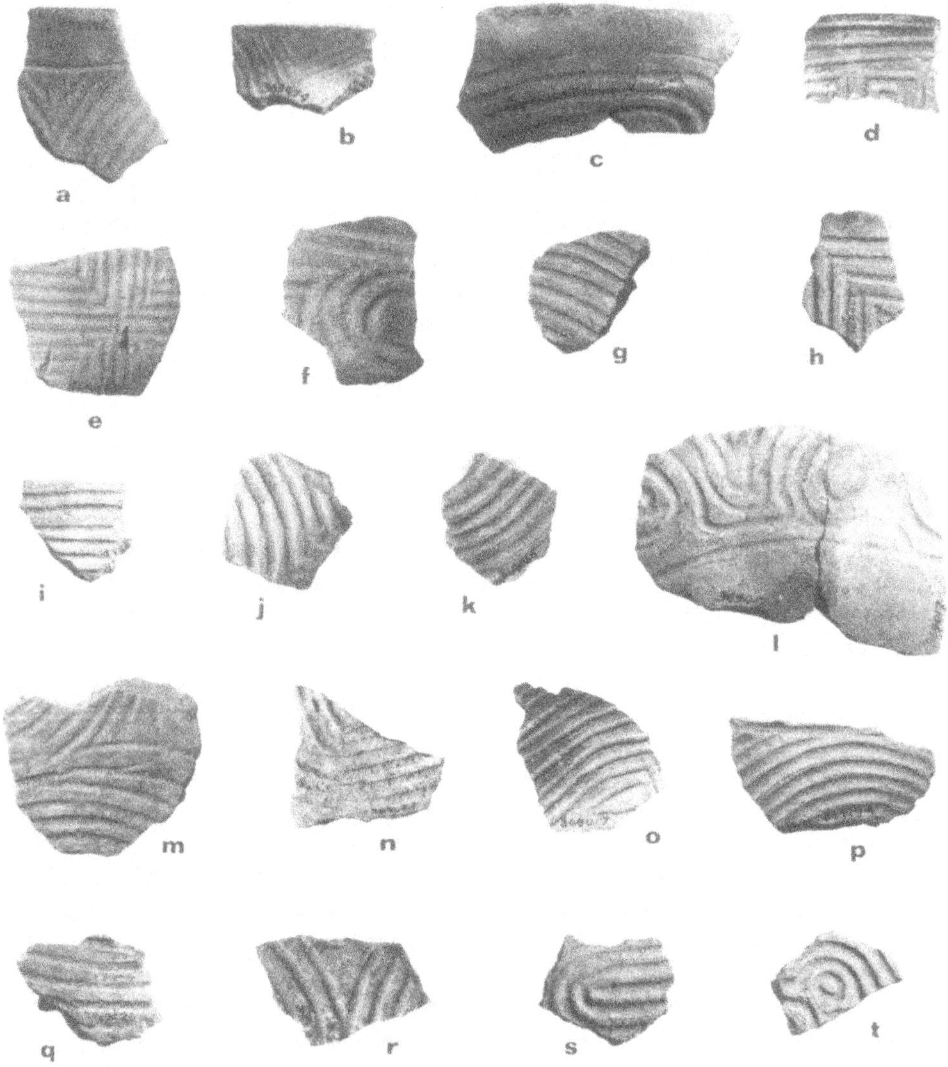

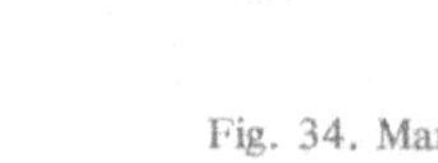

PROVENIENCE: A, CUT D/4; B,C,E,F,H,K,M,N,S HOUSE A; D,L,O MOUND 4; G,P,T VILLAGE SURFACE; I, CUT A/2; J, CUT D/3; Q, CUT F/1; R, TRENCH D/A-B

Fig. 34. Marksville Incised, var. Marksville, close-spaced treatment.

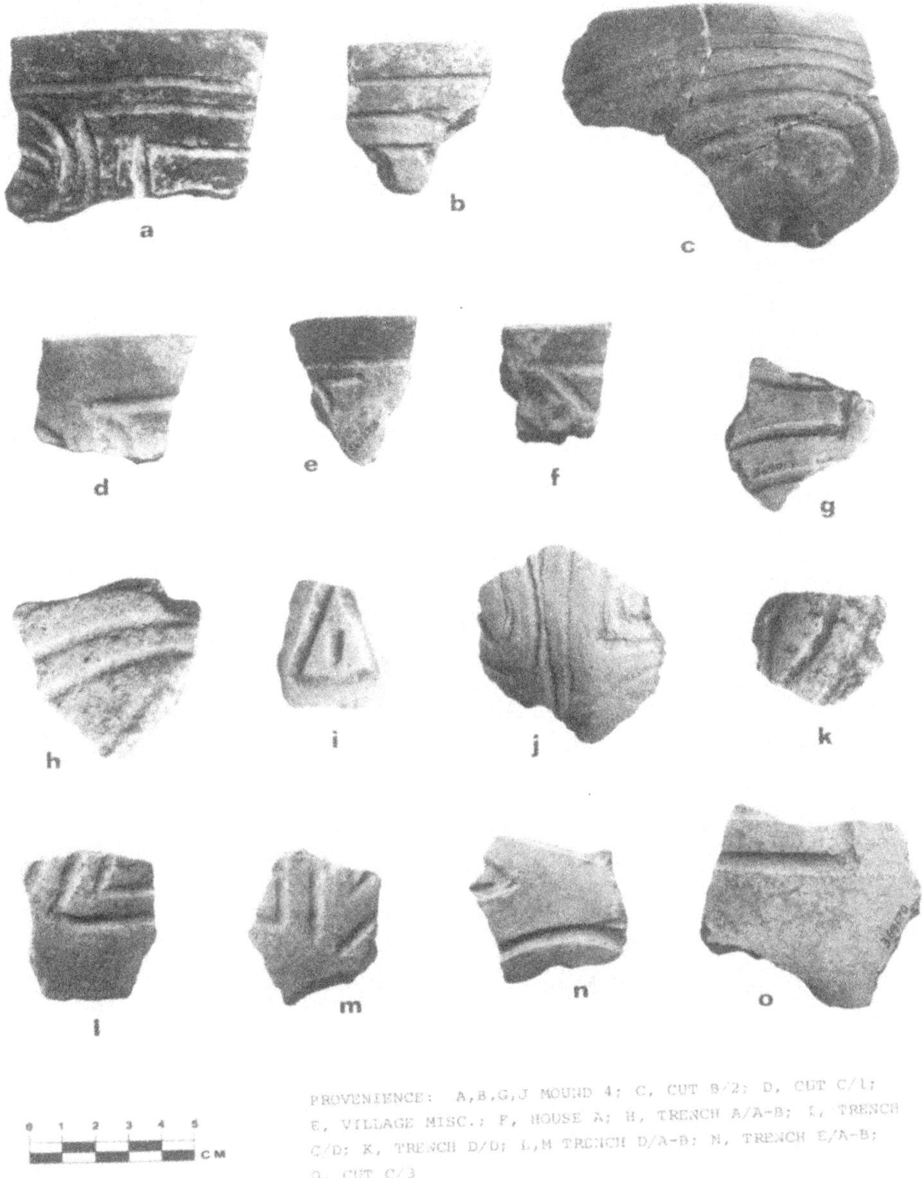

Fig. 35. Marksville Incised, *var. Marksville*, wide-spaced treatment.

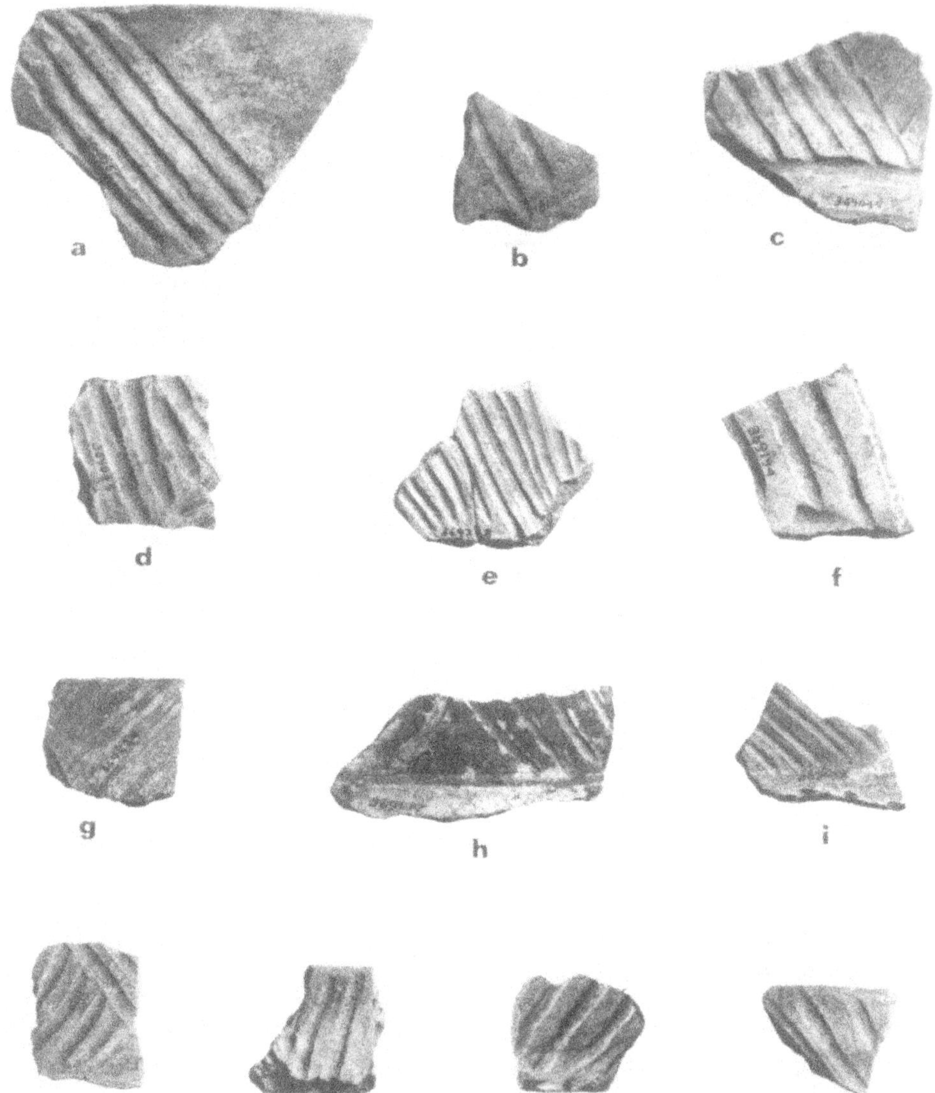

PROVENIENCE: A,B,C,D VILLAGE SURFACE; E,G VILLAGE MISC.; F, CUT D/3; H, MOUND 4; I, CUT A/2; J, HOUSE A; K,M CUT A/1; L, TRENCH C/D

Fig. 36. Marksville Incised, *var.* Marksville, line-filled triangle treatment.

is also a close correspondence between the line-filled triangle treatment of Marksville Incised, *var. Marksville* and the *Goose Lake* variety defined by Phillips (1970:112-13). The two varieties can be separated only by paste differences, but the distinction seems valid since there is nothing to indicate that the line-filled triangle treatment is significantly later than the other two *Marksville* treatments. Most likely, the treatment is simply one that survives into the late Marksville period, and, with modified paste attributes, continues as *Goose Lake* or *Spanish Fort*.

Distribution

The type variety of Marksville Incised, including all three treatments, is found at every known site of the Marksville phase. The variety distribution extends to the Point Lake phase of the Tensas Basin, and it is probable that the classification is valid for early Marksville material from the Yazoo Basin as well. Excellent examples of the close-spaced and wide-spaced treatments, including at least one representation of the broad-billed bird motif, are present in collections from the Dorr site in the Upper Yazoo Basin. Similar material from sites of the Kirk and Anderson Landing phases in the Lower Yazoo Basin would seem to qualify for the *Marksville* variety, but the important paste characteristics of these samples have not been assessed for this study. In any case, it is apparent that early examples of Marksville Incised are broadly similar throughout most of the Lower Mississippi Valley. Whether all of this material can be effectively accommodated by the *Marksville* variety remains to be determined.

Chronological position

The *Marksville* variety of Marksville Incised is securely dated to the early Marksville period. Association with the Hopewellian derived crosshatched rim and bird design attests to such a correlation for the close- and wide-spaced treatments. The line-filled triangle treatment, now confirmed only for the Marksville phase, appears to be coeval, but future research may prove that it is a slightly later development, perhaps one that coincides with the degeneration and eventual disappearance of the Marksville rims.

Marksville Incised, *var. Yokena*
(Figure 37*a-k*)

The *Yokena* sample from the Marksville site, amounting to only about thirty-six sherds, is insufficient to amplify upon the excellent variety description offered by Phillips (1970:117-19). At Marksville, the *Yokena* is

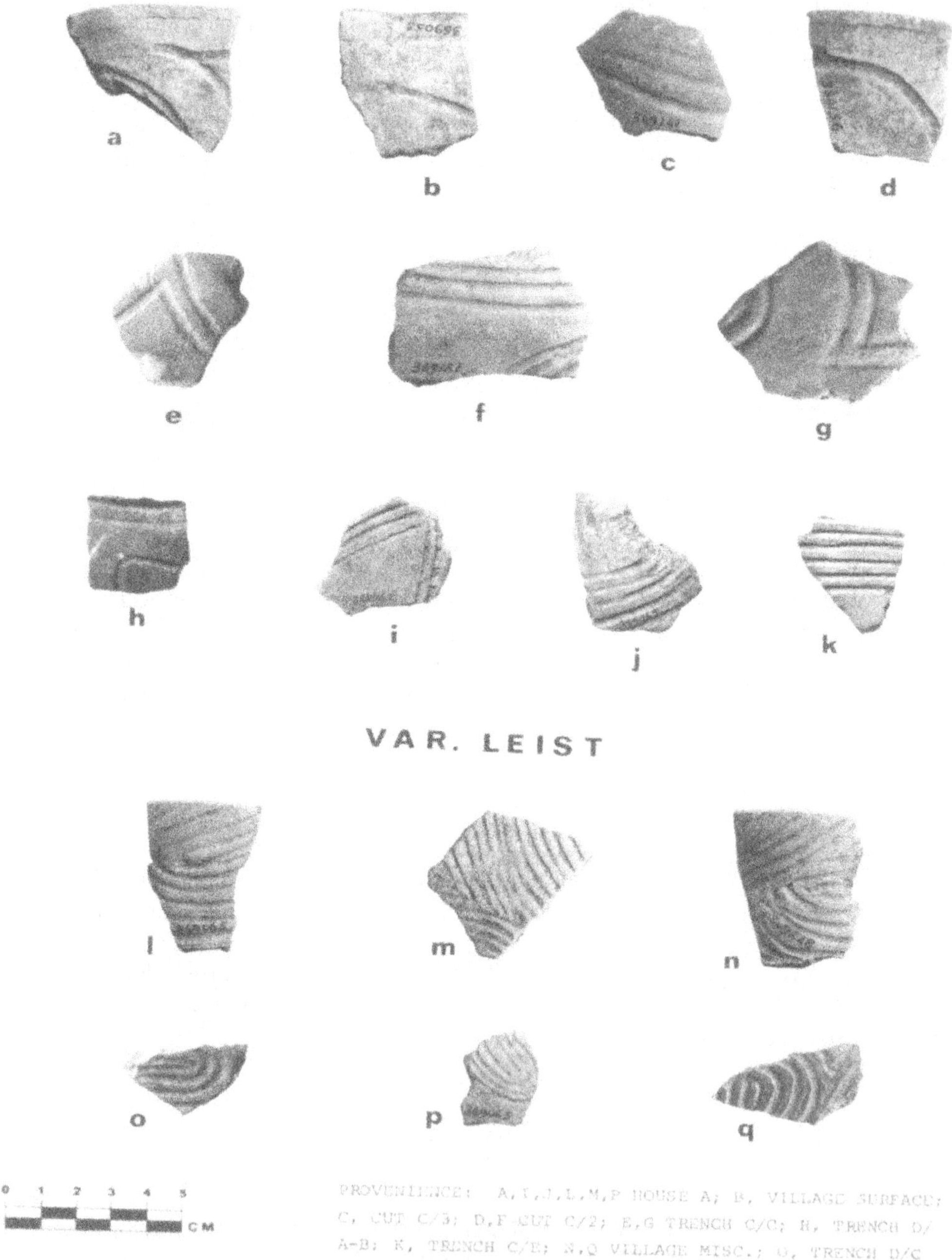

Fig. 37. Marksville Incised, var. Yokena and Marksville incised, var. Leist.

characterized by a compact paste, approaching that of the *Satartia* variety of Baytown Plain, and it is significantly harder, cleaner, and thinner than the pottery of the Marksville phase. The average thickness is 4 to 5 mm. As can be seen in Figure 37*a-k*, the *Yokena* at Marksville corresponds in decoration to that defined by Phillips. Broad U-shaped lines are incised on a smooth surface in both curvilinear and rectilinear designs. The "Two-line Circle" motif is present. The sample includes both wide- and close-spaced treatments. On the Marksville Prairie, *Yokena* is a marker for the Baptiste phase.

Marksville Incised, *var. Leist*
(Figure 37*l-q*)

Only six sherds in the Marksville site collections are classified as *Leist* and, again, nothing can be added to the existing variety description (Phillips, 1970:113-14).The sherds are all 4 to 5 mm thick and made of the compact paste that is characteristic of the Baptiste phase. Decoration consists of neatly executed parallel incised lines arranged in a curvilinear loop design that is somewhat reminiscent of a fingerprint.

Marksville Stamped, *var. Marksville*
(Figure 38)

Nearly half of the decorated ceramics in all collections attributable to the Marksville phase can be classified as the type variety of Marksville Stamped. This diagnostic and very popular decoration is found on ware comparable to that described as Baytown Plain, *var. Marksville*. The soft, thick, chalky pottery averages 7 mm in thickness, with most sherds falling between 6 and 8 mm. Surfaces of *Marksville* sherds are often badly eroded, thus making it extremely hard to assess the fine decorative details without well-aimed side lighting. The variety description is based on large samples of similar material from the Marksville and Crooks sites, but identical ceramics can be found at all sites of the Marksville phase.

Sorting criteria

Broad, deep, U-shaped incised lines are used to delineate design elements which are then emphasized by roughening of the background by dentate rocker stamping. More rarely, the background is left plain and the design itself is roughened in the same manner. Despite efforts to isolate distinct treatments within *Marksville*, the variety continues to include a considerable range in the size of the dentate stamp and the breadth of the rocker stamping. Both

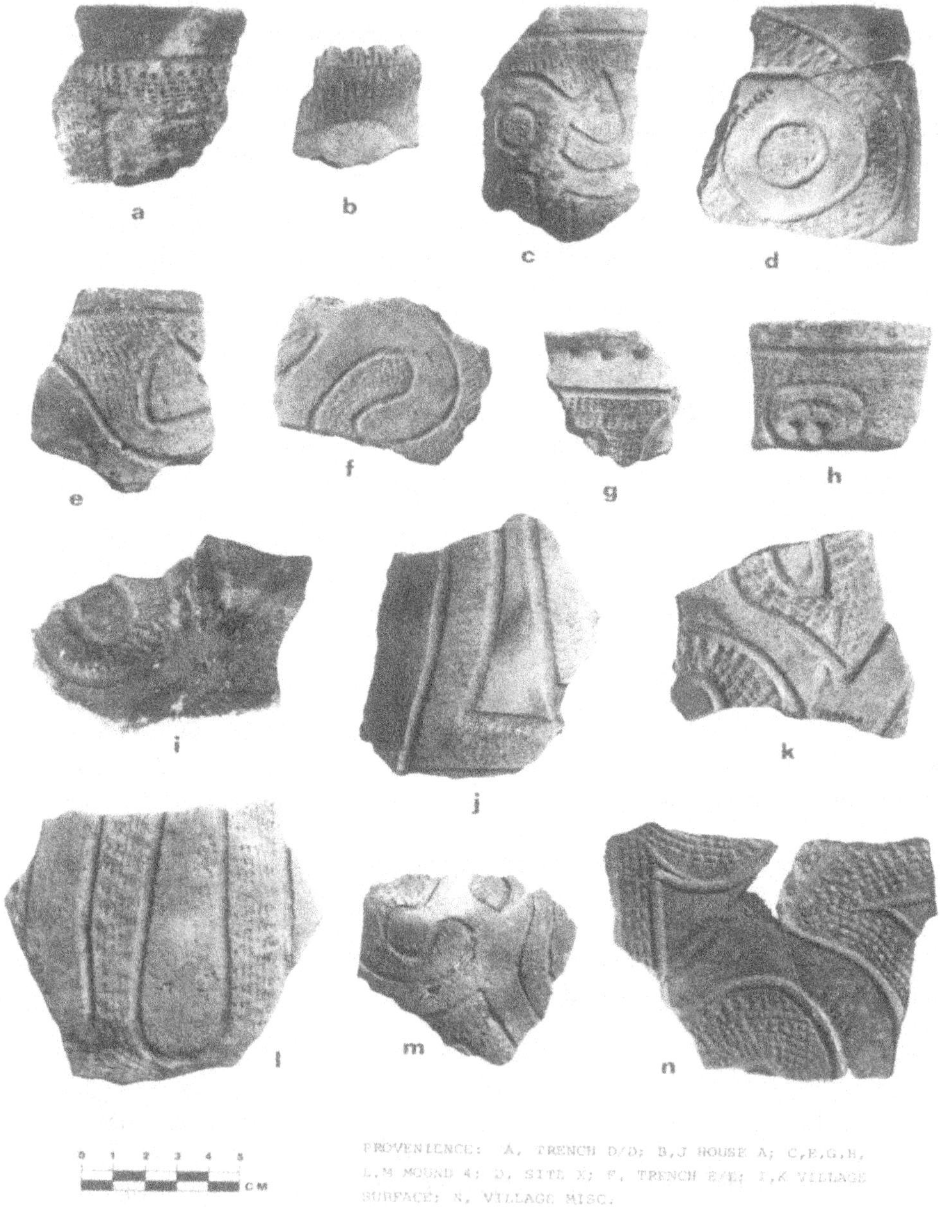

PROVENIENCE: A, TRENCH D/D; B,J HOUSE A; C,E,G,H, L,M MOUND 4; D, SITE X; F, TRENCH E/E; I,K VILLAGE SURFACE; N, VILLAGE MISC.

Fig. 38. Marksville Stamped, var. Marksville.

variables seem to be partly a function of the size of the zone to be filled. Normally, the rocker stamping is rather bold and is executed with a notched instrument having medium to large teeth. In low frequency, however, both tight zigzags and fine dentate stamping are present in most *Marksville* samples.

Virtually all design motifs of the Marksville phase are associated with the *Marksville* variety. The most diagnostic motifs—especially within but not limited to the class of mortuary vessels—include the Hopewellian-inspired raptorial and broad-billed birds, and the vertically bisected circle. Sets of undivided concentric circles, rings of which are alternately roughened, constitute another very common motif. The same principle of alternating plain and roughened bands is used in a number of other simple designs featuring vertical, horizontal, and V-shaped arrangements. The *Marksville* variety is also characterized by a wide range of complex meandering designs in which looping and branching bands are the major elements.

The full spectrum of Marksville vessel modes are found in the type variety of Marksville Stamped. On vessel forms which have undifferentiated rims, namely the small beakers and the bowls, the body decoration generally continues right to the lip or to a narrow plain rim band. Vessel forms with constricted necks, and hence a well-defined rim zone, more often combine a *Marksville* body decoration with one of the Marksville rim treatments such as crosshatching or vertical incising. This is especially true of the tubby pots which demonstrate a very high correlation with the Marksville rim treatments. In fact, the *Marksville* variety is often combined with a tubby pot form, a crosshatched Marksville rim, and a raptorial bird motif to yield what is probably the most diagnostic example of Marksville ceramics.

Analysis of the very large *Marksville* samples from Marksville and Crooks suggests, finally, an intuitive measure of continuity between the type variety and the succeeding *Manny* and *Newsome* varieties of the Baptiste phase. Most of the sherds classified as *Marksville* have the unmistakable soft, chalky paste associated with the Marksville phase. Examples of the bird motif and the vertically bisected circle fall into this soft paste category. Some of the *Marksville* material, however, exhibits a slightly harder, cleaner paste which begins to grade into that found with *Manny* and *Newsome*. Concentric circles and alternating plain and roughened band motifs predominate in the improved paste *Marksville* sub-sample. With better contextual control, it should be possible to demonstrate a gradual transition from *Marksville* to the zoned dentate stamped varieties of the Baptiste phase. A parallel situation is likely between Marksville incised, *var. Marksville* and *Yokena*. Improved paste, lesser thickness, and changes in prevailing design motifs document the transition in both cases.

Distribution

The distribution of Marksville Stamped, *var. Marksville* parallels that of the type variety of Marksville Incised. It is definitely a major constituent of the Marksville and Point Lake phase ceramic complexes in the Lower Red River and Tensas regions, and the variety is probably shared by early Marksville phases in the Yazoo Basin.

Chronological position

The *Marksville* variety of Marksville Stamped is a marker for the early Marksville period, especially when associated with the bird motif or a Marksville rim. As presently defined, the variety persists through the entire time span of the Marksville phase with few recognizable changes. It should be noted, however, that in earlier Marksville phase contexts the type variety appears to be equalled in frequency by *Mabin* and *Crooks*; in later contexts it is matched by *Troyville*. Thus, on the Marksville Prairie and in surrounding environs, very high percentages of *Marksville* in relation to other Marksville Stamped varieties may indicate a narrower temporal position equivalent to the middle portion of the Marksville phase continuum.

Marksville Stamped, *var. Crooks*
(Figure 39)

The most distinctive variety of Marksville Stamped is found in low frequency at all sites of the Marksville phase. *Crooks* is so easy to recognize that one is tempted, in view of the "rule of sortability" (Phillips, 1970:26), to restore the variety to type status. Nothing would be gained by such a maneuver, however, for *Crooks* is a minority decoration in all contexts and quite sensibly accommodated as a variety of Marksville Stamped. *Crooks* is normally matched with a soft Marksville paste, but there are several extremely fine exceptions in the set of mortuary vessels from the Crooks site. The variety also deviates from other Marksville phase ceramics in having a mean thickness of only four to five mm.

Sorting criteria

As with other Marksville Stamped varieties, designs are zoned by wide U-shaped incised lines. The background is roughened by application of the edge of a small shell, presumably a scallop shell. The shell stamping is not rocked, and the individual wavy lines are predominantly close-spaced. To some degree, the size of the shell undulations is matched to the size of the zone to be filled.

The *Crooks* variety does not appear to be associated with the full range of Marksville vessel modes. Thus far, it is limited to ovoid and hemispherical

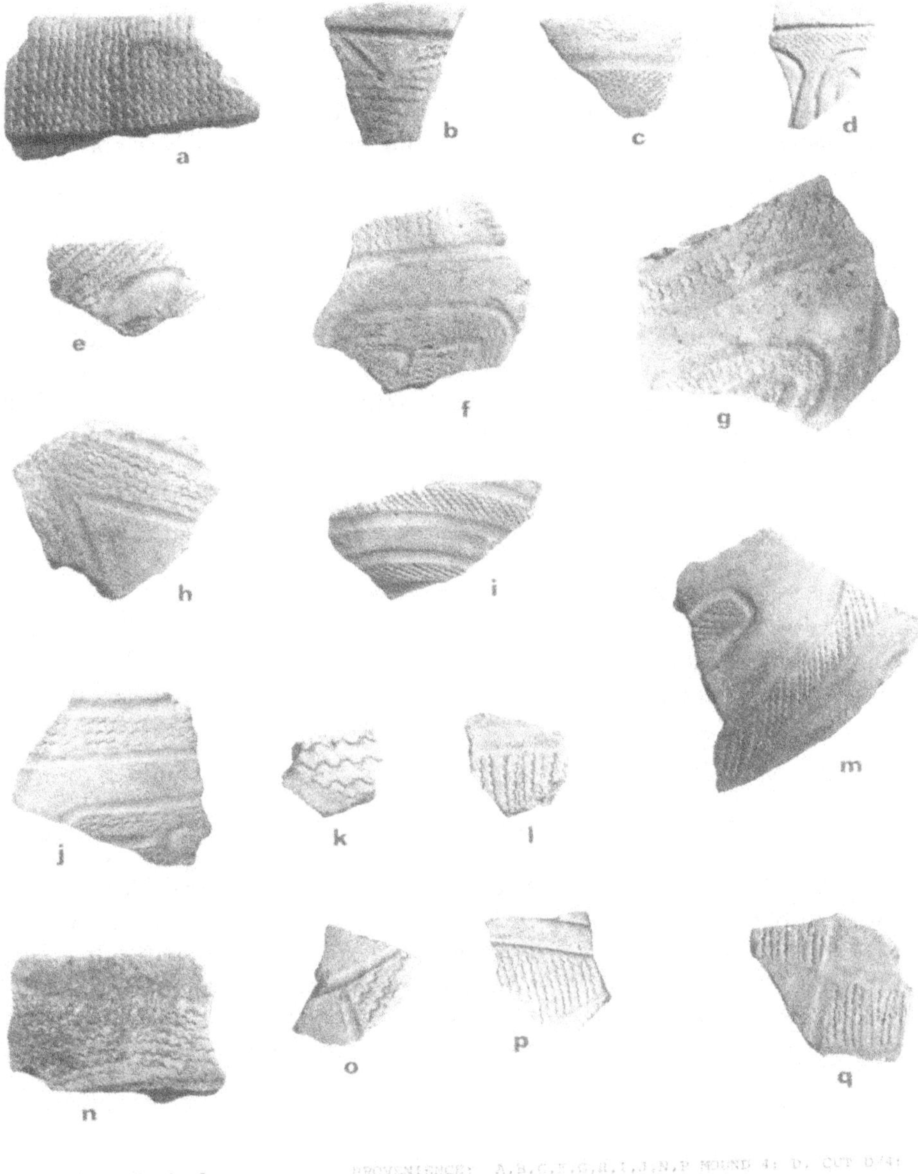

PROVENIENCE: A,B,C,E,G,H,I,J,N,P MOUND 4; D, CUT D/4; F,M,Q HOUSE A; K,L VILLAGE SURFACE; O, CUT A/?

Fig. 39. Marksville Stamped, *var.* Crooks

bowls, and to the irregular "boat-shaped" and "boot-shaped" forms. Design motifs include the raptorial bird as well as alternating plain and roughened bands in curvilinear or rectilinear arrangements. Normally, the body decoration stops at a plain narrow rim band. There are no known associations with the crosshatched or other Marksville rim treatments, but one of these is paralleled by lines of vertical shell stamping on the rim. Shell stamping is also found on top of a wide, flat lip.

Distribution

As presently known, the northern limit of the *Crooks* variety is the Crooks site in Catahoula Parish. It is found at all sites of the Marksville phase, in southern Louisiana, and eastward along the Gulf coast. Its presence, apparently in late contexts, at several Tchefuncte sites in the Lake Pontchartrain region is noteworthy. Ford and Quimby (1945) document such provenience at the Tchefuncte, Little Woods, and Big Oak Island sites.

Chronological position

Where found, *Crooks* is one of the best markers for the early Marksville period. At Marksville phase sites, the variety seems to reach a peak in popularity very early. It thus joins *Mabin* as one of the earliest diagnostics of the Marksville phase.

Marksville Stamped, *var. Mabin*
(Figure 40)

Although a minority decoration at Marksville, the *Mabin* variety appears to be one of the most important indicators of a certain early Marksville affiliation. The variety combines a number of decorative treatments which can also be found in Havana Zoned Stamped ceramics of the Illinois Valley. *Mabin* is accompanied by the soft, chalky paste described for Baytown Plain, *var. Marksville*, and sherds average 6 to 7 mm in thickness.

Sorting criteria

Designs are outlined by the usual wide U-shaped incised lines and then highlighted by background roughening. As presently defined, the background roughening in *Mabin* is accomplished by a number of distinct decorative treatments including parallel rows of cord-wrapped stick impressions, straight dentate impressions, crescent dentate stamping, rows of individual cord impressions, and curved dentate stamping. Only two of these, the cord-

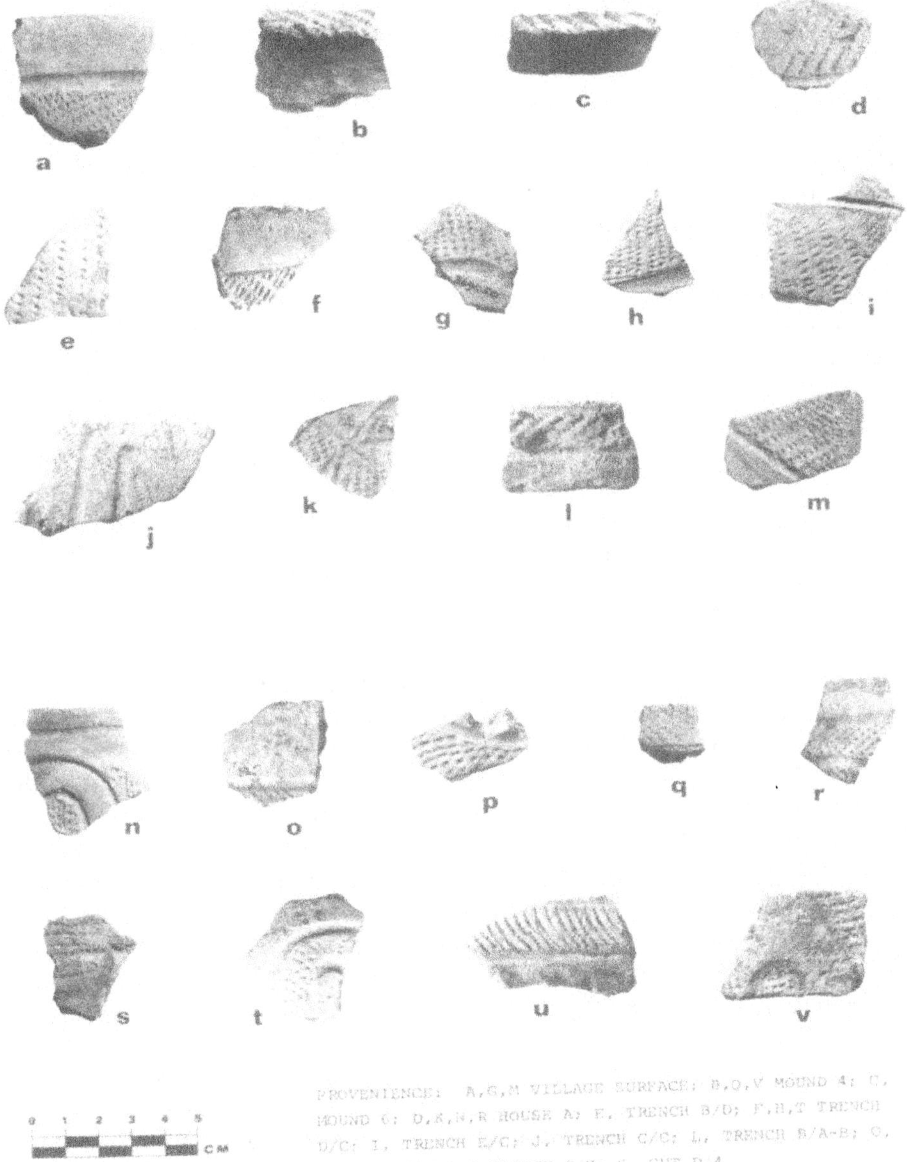

Fig. 40. Marksville Stamped, var. Mabin, Cord-wrapped stick treatment and Straight Dentate Treatment.

wrapped stick and straight dentate treatments, are present in the Marksville site collections. However, all the treatments can be found in samples from the Norman site in the northeastern corner of the Lower Mississippi Valley and at sites in southern Mississippi County, Missouri. Moreover, in these northern regions the treatments are sometimes combined with zones of red filming. Griffin's suggestion that *Mabin* should be restored to type status (Griffin, 1973:377) is, therefore, very convincing, and it is quite likely that forthcoming analysis of the Norman material will result in such modification. If *Mabin* is elevated to type status, the six or more treatments now recognized within *Mabin* would in turn be defined as varieties. The change would thus limit the type Marksville Stamped to zoned rocker stamping.

The *Mabin* variety is associated with the raptorial bird motif, the vertically bisected circle, alternately roughened bands in V-shaped and other simple arrangements, and with a strange motif (see Ford and Willey, 1940: Fig. 30*a*) that is highly suggestive of a sprouting plant. *Mabin* vessel forms include at least the tubby pot, small beakers, and straight jars. The cross-hatched and other Marksville rims are sometimes associated with *Mabin*, but more often the decoration stops at a plain upper rim band.

Cord-wrapped stick treatment.—In the Lower Red River and Tensas regions, the most plentiful *Mabin* treatment consists of zoned cord-wrapped stick impressions (Fig. 40*a-m*). The parallel rows of impressions show that the cord-wrapped stick was lifted between applications rather than rocked. Normally, the *Mabin* cord-wrapped stick impressions are rather fine as in the Hopewell style of the Illinois Valley. An excellent comparison is furnished by the Hopewell Zoned Stamped, cord-wrapped stick variety, vessel from Mound 5 at the Gibson site in Calhoun County, Illinois (Perino, 1968: Fig. 52). The larger cord-wrapped stick impressions of the Havana style are also paralleled, however, as can be seen on two *Mabin* vessels from Crooks (Ford and Willey, 1940: Figs. 28*c*, 34). The treatment is frequently used to decorate rims of *Mabin* vessels, cord-wrapped stick impressions being applied on the top of a broad, flat lip or around the rim band in parallel rows that are slanted roughly forty-five degrees to one side.

Straight dentate treatment.—A denticulated stamp is also used to fill zones on *Mabin* vessels (Fig. 40*n-v*). The stamp is notched to create a line of rectangular teeth that are aligned end to end. A similar tool, when rocked, may result in the type variety of Marksville Stamped. In the *Mabin* straight dentate treatment, however, the stamp is lifted and reapplied to generate lines of dentate impressions. Often there is a slight size difference between adjacent teeth, and a distinct pattern of teeth can be seen to repeat from line to line.

Distribution

At sites of the Marksville phase, *Mabin* is found in low frequency, and only the cord-wrapped stick and straight dentate treatments are represented. *Mabin* is much more abundant at sites of the Point Lake phase in the Tensas region, and a similar pattern can be expected in the Anderson Landing and Dorr phases of the Yazoo Basin. As mentioned previously, the full range of *Mabin* treatments is present at the Norman site where the variety appears to occupy a very prominent position in the ceramic complex. Further research will probably establish that *Mabin* applies to early phases across the entire Lower Mississippi Valley.

Chronological position

There is considerable evidence that *Mabin* is one of the earliest Marksville decorations. It is a firm marker for the early Marksville period. At the Marksville site, *Mabin* is the deepest variety found in the trenches around Mound 2, and in other early contexts it equals or surpasses the type variety of Marksville Stamped. The parallels between *Mabin* treatments and Havana varieties in the Illinois Valley also point to an early date. However, it must be recognized that *Mabin* resembles the Hopewell style and incorporates the Hopewellian bird design and crosshatched rim. Therefore, one can hypothesize that *Mabin*—and Hopewellian influence in general—entered the Lower Mississippi Valley around the time that the Havana style is joined by the Hopewell style in the Illinois Valley.

Marksville Stamped, *var. Troyville*
(Figure 41)

If associations in the Marksville ceramic collections can be trusted, plain zoned rocker stamping has a longer life span than formerly suspected and may persist throughout the entire Marksville period. Efforts to divide the *Troyville* of the Marksville and Baptiste phases into separate varieties have thus far been unsuccessful, primarily because the only recognized attribute distinctions pertain to paste characteristics. More thorough analysis of samples from the Baptiste site may still isolate the necessary, but elusive, variables. Most of the material from the Marksville site that is here classified as *Troyville* averages 6 mm in thickness and is made with the soft, chalky paste characteristic of the Marksville phase. However, unaccompanied by pronounced changes in design or execution, a small percentage of the *Troyville* at Marksville is thinner and has the compact paste associated with the Baptiste phase. Overall, the "improved" *Troyville* grades into the equivalent of the original material from the Troyville site (Walker, 1936: Plate 12*e-k*).

PROVENIENCE: A, TRENCH C/A-B; B,E,H,L,M HOUSE A; C,F CUT C/1; D, VILLAGE MISC.; G, CUT C/3; I, TRENCH B/C; J,K VILLAGE SURFACE; N, CUT A/1

Fig. 41. Marksville Stamped, var. Troyville

Sorting criteria

Wide, deep, U-shaped lines are used to outline zones of plain rocker stamping. Very little of the "pseudo-dentate" rocker stamping described by Phillips (1970:126) is included in the *Troyville* counts from Marksville, although it is possible that some of the Marksville Stamped, *var. Marksville* with an eroded surface might qualify for such a treatment. The plain rocker stamping normally runs in a continuous series of zigzags, the direction of application being parallel to the orientation of the band being filled (Fig. 41*b,c,h,n*); occasionally, however, the zigzags are applied in short lengths that are perpendicular to the zoning lines (Fig. 41*d,i,m*). The roughened bands are usually fairly wide—on the average 2 to 3 cm across—and, in turn, widely separated. All of the sherds illustrated in Figure 41 are examples of the soft, chalky *Troyville* which presumably is associated with the Marksville phase.

In the main, *Troyville* is used with the alternating plain and roughened bands motif. Such arrangements tend to be simple and more rectilinear than curvilinear or triangular. Long filled ovals are another fairly common *Troyville* motif. So far, there is no indication that *Troyville* is associated with either the bird design or the vertically bisected circle. Similarly, there is no positive association with the Marksville crosshatched, vertically incised, or slanted incised rim treatments. Most often, the *Troyville* decoration stops at a plain rim band set off by a single incised line. Nevertheless, at least two diagnostic Marksville rim treatments can be found with the Troyville variety: the dash-dot treatment (Fig. 26*b*) and the plain band treatment which is demarcated by a row of hemiconical punctates and sometimes an incised line.

Distribution

To date, the soft paste *Troyville* is confirmed only at Marksville phase sites in the Lower Red River region. A small *Troyville* sample from the Point Lake site in the Tensas region may be comparable, but it is unknown whether or not the distinction can be extended further north into the Yazoo Basin. The range of *Troyville* made with the harder, more compact paste like that of the *Satartia* variety of Baytown Plain does, of course, include the southern portion of the Yazoo Basin as well as the Tensas and Lower Red River regions.

Chronological position

Until an early zoned plain rocker stamped variety can be isolated and linked with specific phases, the *Troyville* variety, as used here, is not an effective temporal indicator. Superficially at least, it seems apparent that *Troyville* decoration combined with soft paste points to an early Marksville period identification. Conversely, the *Troyville* with improved paste belongs to the middle and late portions of the Marksville period. In general, it would seem that zoned plain rocker stamping increases in popularity toward the end of the Marksville period.

Marksville Stamped, *var. Manny* (Figure 42*a-k*)

The *Manny* sample from the Marksville site is too small to suggest refinements to the existing variety description (Phillips, 1970:123-25). At Marksville, *Manny* can be distinguished from Marksville phase ceramics by a harder, cleaner paste that resembles the *Satartia* variety of Baytown Plain. Sherds range from 4 to 5 mm in thickness. In general, the *Manny* at Marksville corresponds quite closely to that described for Issaquena sites. Medium to coarse dentate rocker stamping is applied in wide zigzags to fill zones created by broad U-shaped lines. The execution of the dentate rocker stamping is often neater than is the case with the type variety of Marksville Stamped. Designs tend to be repetitive and involve simple motifs such as alternately roughened circles, triangles, and loops. Although the sample is small, it seems sufficient to confirm that, as in the Tensas and Yazoo basins, *Manny* is not associated with the bird motif or the Marksville rim treatments. On the Marksville Prairie, *Manny* is a marker for the Baptiste phase which is assumed to date to the middle to late Marksville period.

Marksville Stamped, *var. Newsome* (Figure 42*l-s*)

As in the case of the other Baptiste phase varieties, there are not enough *Newsome* sherds in the Marksville collections to justify changes or supplements to the existing variety description (Phillips, 1970:125). At Marksville, *Newsome* is characterized by compact paste and a thickness range of 4 to 5 mm. The main difference between the decorative treatments of *Manny* and *Newsome* is that the latter features very fine dentate rocker stamping in contrast to the coarser stamping of *Manny*. There is also a tendency for *Newsome* designs to be more complicated, although the variety can be used with fairly simple motifs such as concentric, alternately roughened circles and triangles. The bird motif and Marksville rim treatments are not included in the inventory of *Newsome* decorations. Like *Manny*, the *Newsome* variety of Marksville Stamped is a marker for the Baptiste phase. There is no evidence at Marksville that there is a time difference between the two varieties—such as Phillips (1970:124-25) proposed for the Yazoo Basin—but this may be due to

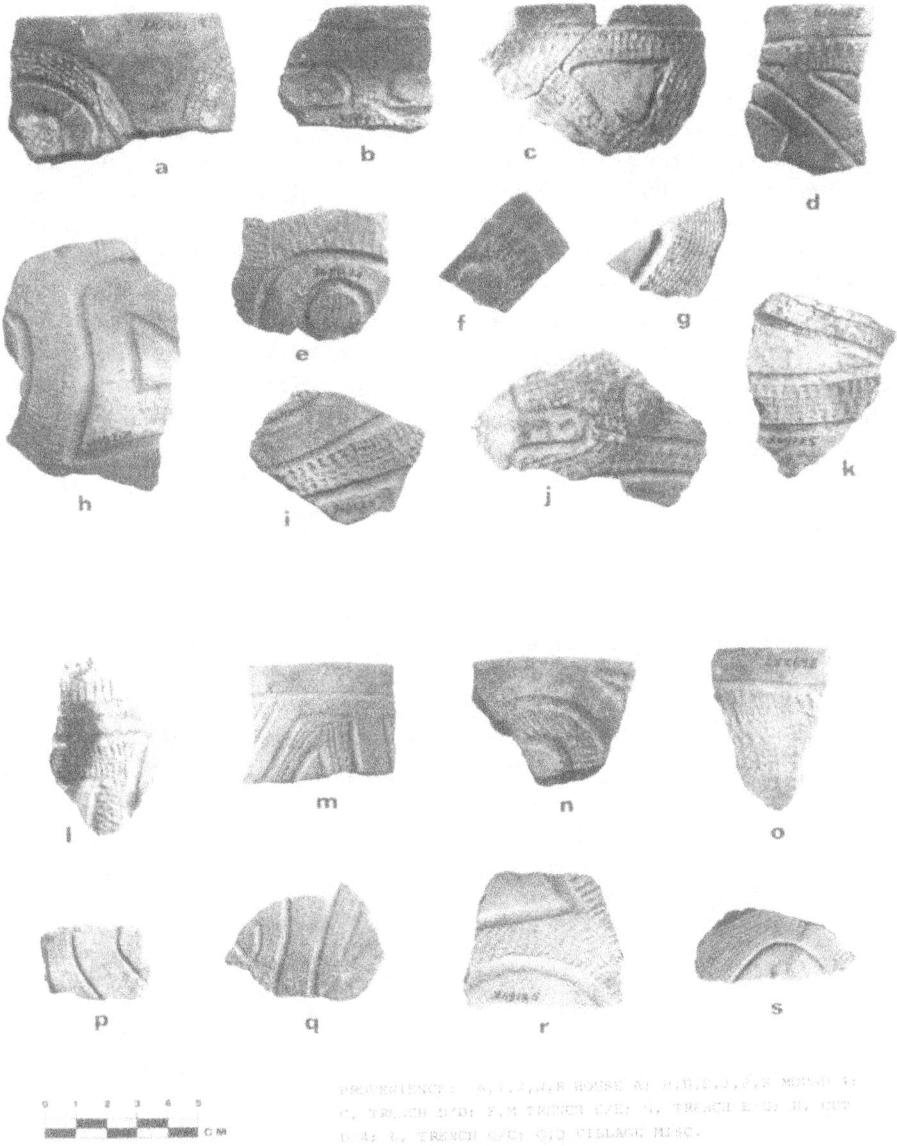

Fig. 42. Marksville Stamped, var. Manny and Marksville Stamped, var. Newsome

sampling error or the lack of provenience specific enough to detect such fine time distinctions.

Indian Bay Stamped, *var. Cypress Bayou*
(Figure 43*a-e*)

The type Indian Bay Stamped is very poorly represented in the Marksville collections, but at least two varieties are present. An unzoned, plain rocker stamped variety is listed in the ceramic counts as Indian Bay Stamped, *var. unspecified*. With respect to existing variety descriptions (Phillips, 1970:91-93), the treatment seems to fall somewhere in between the *Shaw* and *Indian Bay* varieties, but the sample is much too poor to elaborate or even to illustrate. The other Indian Bay Stamped variety at Marksville features unzoned dentate rocker stamping and is classified as the *Cypress Bayou* variety. Since *Cypress Bayou* seems to be a minority constituent of the Marksville ceramic complex, a few brief comments are offered to bolster the variety description provided by Phillips (1970:91-92). The description is based on a mere handful of sherds from the Marksville site collections.

Sorting criteria

The main distinction of the *Cypress Bayou* variety is that the decoration is unzoned and used as an allover treatment. Dentate rocker stamping is applied in unzoned parallel bands which may be oriented on the vessel either vertically or horizontally. The width of the plain space between the bands of rocker stamping varies considerably. Similarly, the tightness of the rocker stamping in the Marksville sample varies from very closely spaced zigzags approaching those on the beautifully executed vessel from Crooks (Ford and Willey, 1940: Fig. 31*b*) to quite open zigzags as paralleled by sherds from the northern Yazoo Basin (Phillips et al., 1951: Fig. 80*k,p*). In both cases, the *Cypress Bayou* is matched with a soft, chalky paste identical to that described as Baytown Plain, *var. Marksville*.

Distribution

Thus far, *Cypress Bayou* is identified only at the Marksville and Crooks sites in the Lower Red River region. However, the two sherds illustrated in the first survey volume (Phillips et al., 1951: Fig. 80*k,p*) would seem to qualify as *Cypress Bayou*, thereby suggesting a considerably greater range.[14]

[14] Good examples of the *Cypress Bayou* variety are present at the Rochdale site in Bolivar County, Mississippi. This newly discovered site in the northern Yazoo Basin has a rich early Marksville component which suggests many ceramic ties to sites of the Marksville and Point Lake phases.

Fig. 43. Indian Bay Stamped, var. Cypress Bayou and Mulberry Creek Cord Marked, var. Sevier.

Quite possibly, the variety has been overlooked in the other regions by assuming that the zoning lines of one of the Marksville Stamped varieties were simply missing.

Chronological position

Provenience in the Marksville site collections suggests that *Cypress Bayou* is a minority marker of the Marksville phase. The variety is found at Marksville in several contexts that appear to be quite early. A similar identification is supported by an unzoned dentate rocker stamped vessel from Mound A at the Crooks site. The *Cypress Bayou* variety is thus tentatively assigned to the early Marksville period.

Mulberry Creek Cord Marked, *var. Sevier*
(Figure 43*f-o*)

Cord marking of any kind is a rare surface treatment in the Marksville site collections. What there is comes primarily from the surface or from the floor of House A, thereby hinting at the possibility of a Baptiste phase association. However, the cord-marked pottery at Marksville is matched with a soft, chalky paste that belongs to the Marksville, not the Baptiste, phase. A portion of the cord-marked sample features very shallow cord impressions, suggesting no obvious parallels in the Lower Valley, and is listed in the ceramic counts as Mulberry Creek Cord Marked, *var. unspecified*. The remainder of the cord-marked pottery is similar to the *Sevier* variety which has been defined for the Point Lake phase (Toth, 1966:60).

Sorting criteria

The *Sevier* variety of Mulberry Creek Cord Marked is distinguished by very large cord impressions that are applied with a cord-wrapped paddle on ware equivalent to Baytown Plain, *var. Marksville*. The coarse cord marking is often accompanied by a distinctive rim mode that consists basically of inverted notching along the lip which creates a "piecrust" effect when viewed looking down at the lip. The unusually large cord impressions and the rim notching of the *Sevier* variety find parallels in the *Porter Bayou* variety of the southern Yazoo Basin which may be another early Marksville brand of cord marking (Phillips, 1970:138). Nevertheless, the *Sevier* cord impressions are not widely spaced as in *Porter Bayou*, and the soft paste at Marksville does not match the *Reed* variety of Baytown Plain which is required for *Porter Bayou*.

Distribution

The distribution of Mulberry Creek Cord Marked, *var. Sevier* is limited to the Tensas and Lower Red River regions. At Marksville phase sites, cord marking is very rare, but the same is not true for the Point Lake phase. At the Point Lake site, *Sevier* accounts for roughly 20 percent of the total decorated ceramics in collections from an ostensibly pure early Marksville component.

Chronological position

Coarse cord marking appears to be the earliest kind introduced into the Lower Mississippi Valley. When associated with a soft paste, as at Marksville and Point Lake, the resulting *Sevier* variety seems to represent a minority marker for the early Marksville period.

Decorated Rim Modes
(Figures 44-47)

The body decoration of Marksville vessels frequently continues onto the rim zone, and several treatments–such as the *Mabin* cord-wrapped stick impressions and the Marksville Stamped, *var. Marksville* dentate rocker stamping–are even found on top of a wide, flat lip. Such occurrences are noted in the individual variety descriptions. There are also several very distinctive rim treatments that, like modes, crosscut a number of Marksville types and varieties. Since the Marksville rims are extremely diagnostic early Marksville markers, it seems worthwhile to illustrate a sample of the most representative treatments.

Notched rims and lines across lip (Fig. 44)

Although not particularly diagnostic of early Marksville when found alone, notched rims and lines across lips bolster such an identification when associated with the marker varieties. Both can be expected to occur in any early Marksville context. The examples illustrated in Figure 44 are clear-cut and should negate the need for further description.

Marksville rims

Considering that the bird design is often difficult to detect on potsherds, the Marksville rims emerge as probably the most definitive marker for all known phases of the early Marksville period. Most of the Marksville rim

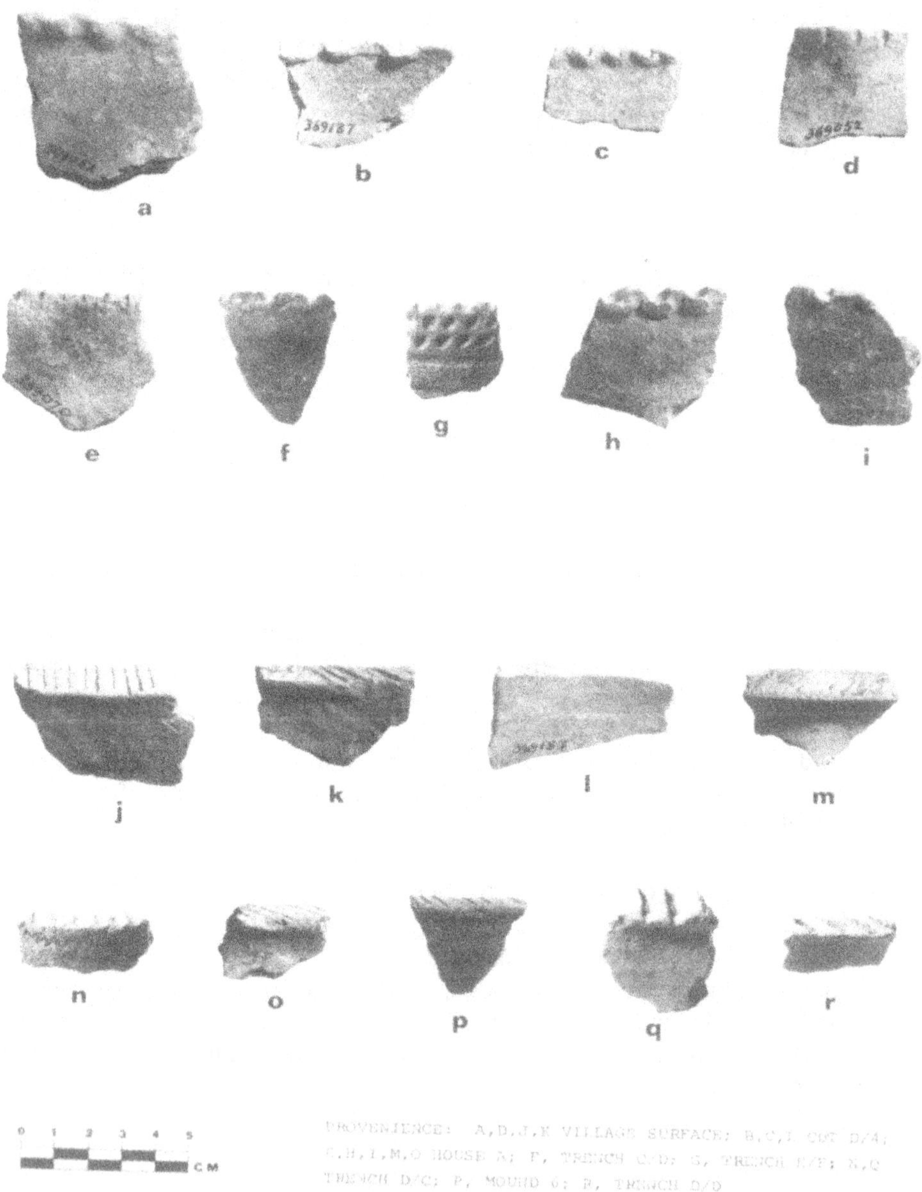

PROVENIENCE: A,D,J,K VILLAGE SURFACE; B,C,L CUT D/4; E,H,I,M,O HOUSE A; F, TRENCH C/D; G, TRENCH E/F; N,Q TRENCH D/C; P, MOUND 6; R, TRENCH D/D

Fig. 44. Notched rims and lines across lip

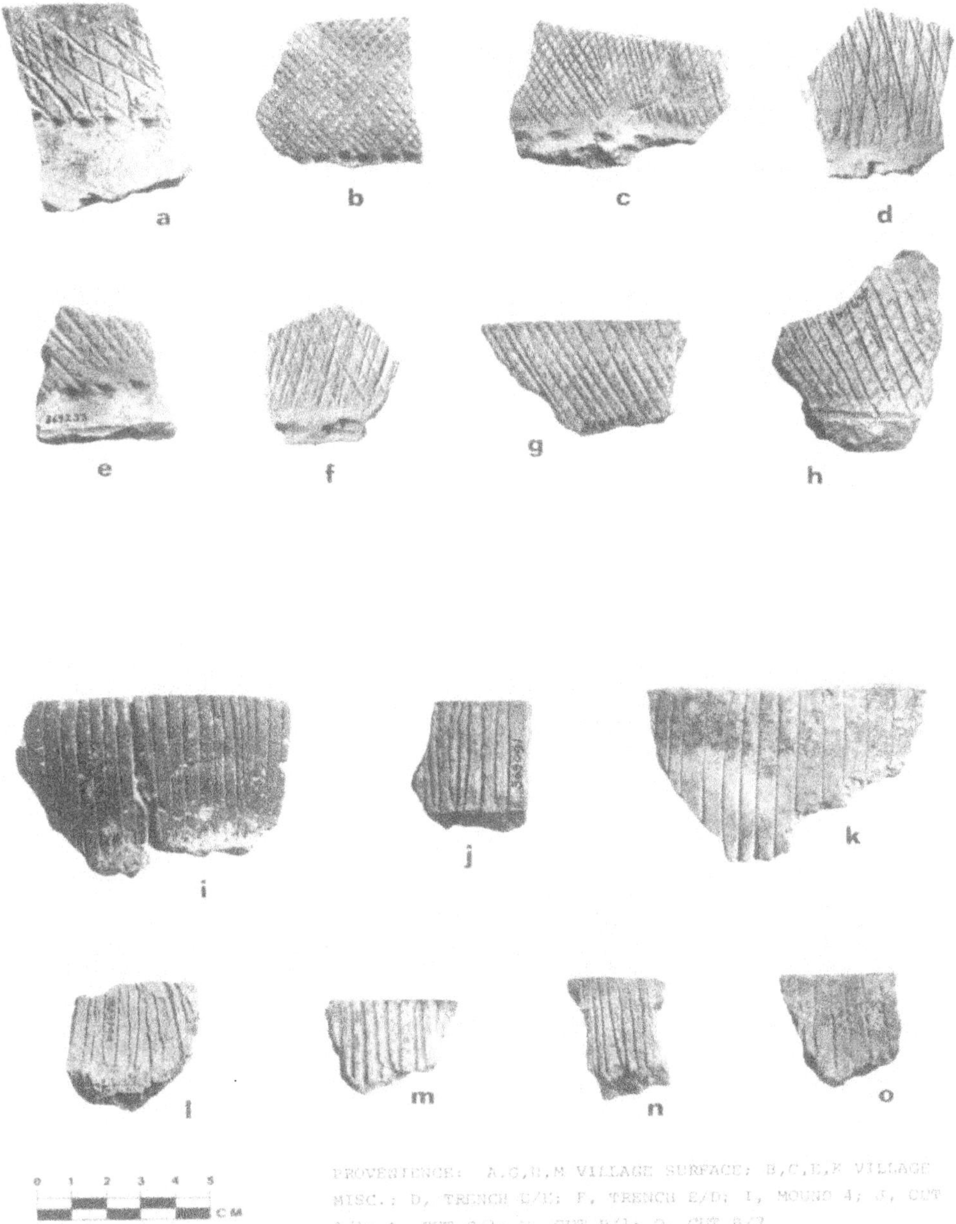

PROVENIENCE: A,G,H,M VILLAGE SURFACE; B,C,E,K VILLAGE MISC.; D, TRENCH E/E; F, TRENCH E/D; I, MOUND 4; J, CUT A/1; L, CUT C/1; N, CUT D/1; O, CUT B/2

Fig. 45. Marksville rims, crosshatched and vertically incised treatments

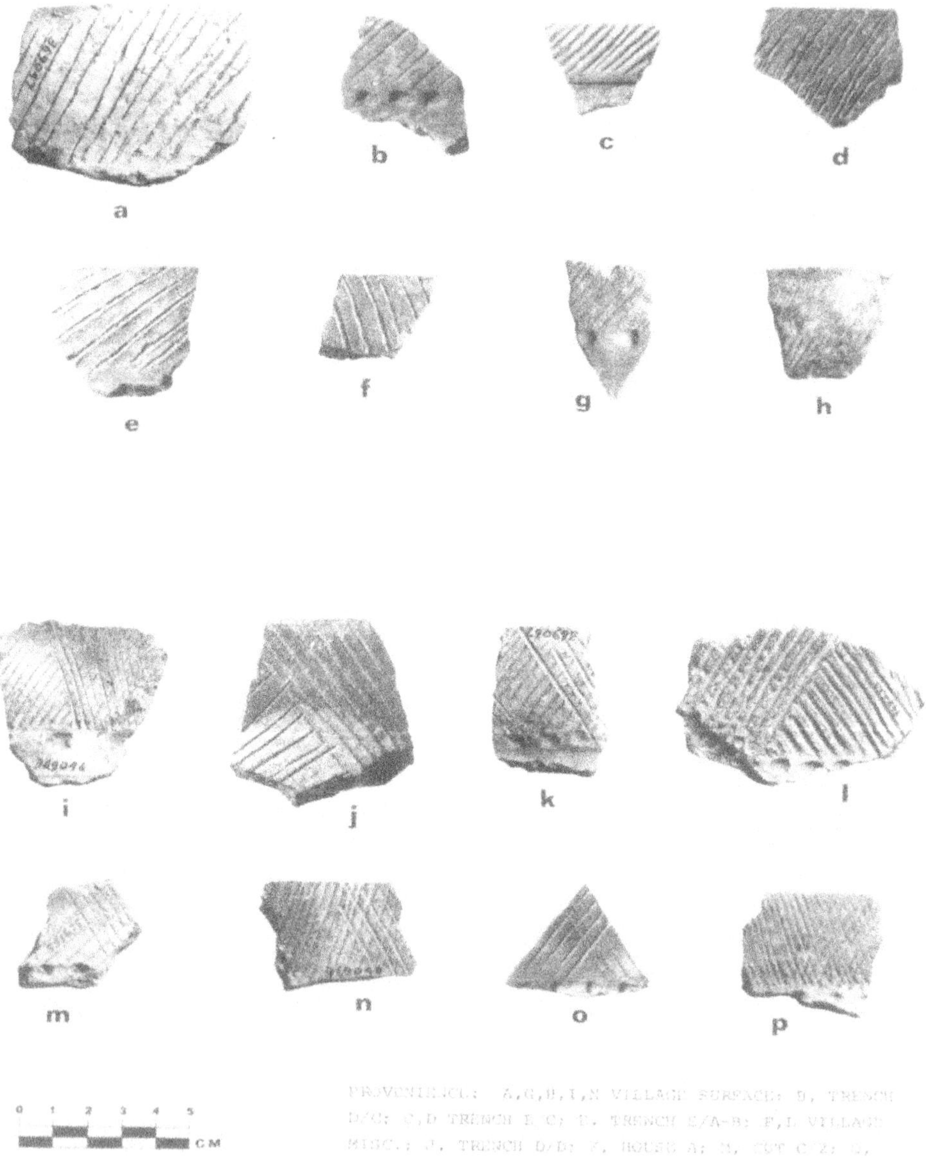

Fig. 46. Marksville rims, slanted incised treatment and alternately slanted treatment

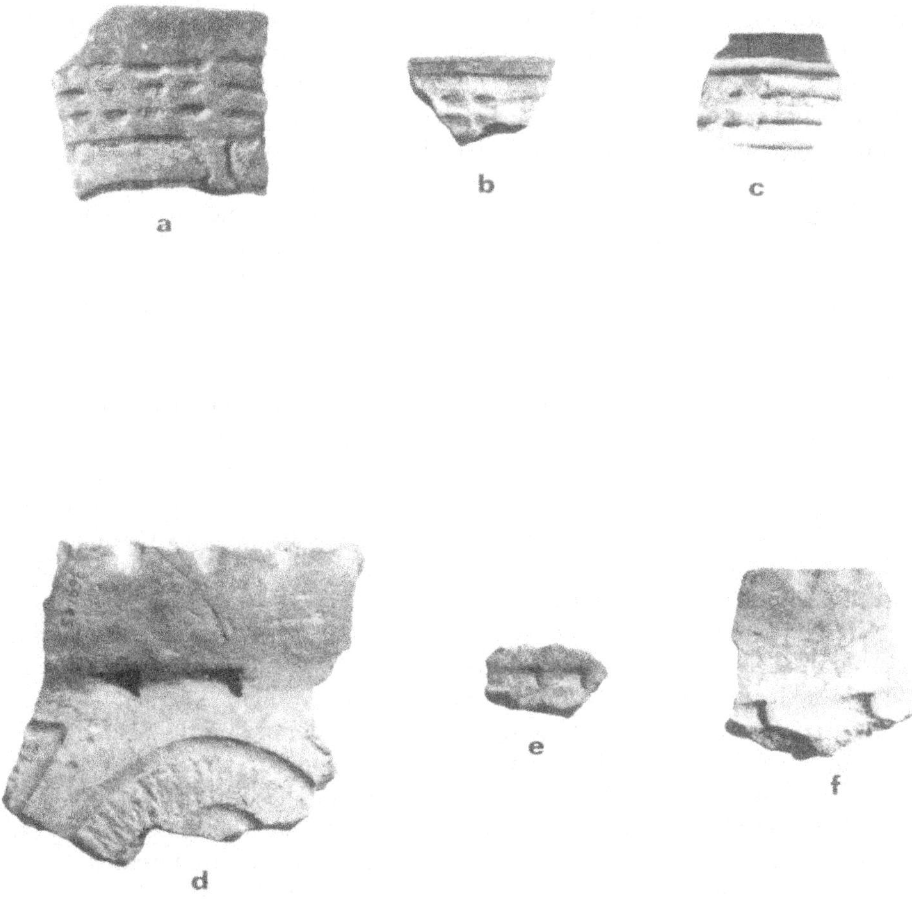

PROVENIENCE: A, TRENCH E/C; B,C MOUND 4; D, CUT C/1;
E, VILLAGE SURFACE; F, CUT D/1

Fig. 47. Marksville rims, dash-dot and plain band treatments

treatments have very obvious parallels in northern Hopewell. Analysis of the Marksville site collections suggests that six distinct treatments can be isolated. Whether or not these six treatments have identical distribution in time and space remains to be determined. For the moment, the six versions of the Marksville rim will be treated individually in hopes that such subdivision will encourage further examination of possible discontinuities in phase associations. The Marksville rims are found most often with the tubby pot vessel mode.

Crosshatched treatment (Fig. 45a-h).—The best known Marksville rim decoration is, of course, the Hopewellian derived crosshatched treatment. It is also the Marksville rim treatment that is found most abundantly, usually in numbers equal to the combined totals of the five other treatments. Fine incised lines are used in a crosshatched decoration covering the rim zone which is normally set off by a broad incised line or a row of hemiconical punctates or both. Occasionally, the crosshatching may be supplemented by notching along the front edge of the lip. Although there are exceptions, in general the execution of the crosshatching is less than neat. There is some indication in the Marksville site collections that the crosshatched treatment may first be applied to a cambered rim with a rounded lip and gradually be adopted to a vertical or outslanted rim with a flat lip that slopes to the inside of the vessel.

Vertically incised treatment (Figure 45i-o).—Equally as diagnostic as crosshatching is a treatment in which fine incised parallel lines are applied vertically to the rim zone. Again, there are northern Hopewell parallels. For example, the identical vertically incised treatment can be seen on a vessel from Mound 1 at the Klunk site in Calhoun County, Illinois (Perino, 1968: Fig. 8). A row of hemiconical punctates or a broad incised line or both usually set off the band of vertical incising.

Slanted incised treatment (Figure 46a-h).—Fine parallel incised lines are also applied to the rim band at roughly a forty-five degree angle. Most often the lines slant to the right, and the spacing between them can vary from quite close to fairly wide. There is normally a broad incised line to demarcate the decorated rim band, but the accompanying hemiconical punctates are used less often than in the other Marksville rim treatments.

Alternately slanted treatment (Figure 46i-p).—The crosshatched and slanted incised treatments are sometimes combined in an alternately slanted treatment. Patches of fine parallel incised lines slant alternately left and right. Where the two orientations merge, a zone of crosshatching results. Less often, the lines are not allowed to overlap and a line-filled triangle motif is formed which, except for the fine lines, is similar to the line-filled triangle treatment of Marksville Incised, *var. Marksville.*

Dash-dot treatment (Figure 47a-c).—Broad U-shaped incised lines are used to mark off the rim zone of Marksville vessels in many ways. The most distinctive application of broad incised lines, however, results when three or four such lines, placed parallel to each other, are periodically interrupted in a dash-dot treatment. The dots, or short jabs of the incising tool, normally number three to a group and are aligned one under the other. The dash-dot treatment may be used to delineate a rim zone of some other decoration, or it may be placed on the rim band itself as a primary decoration. Excellent examples of the dash-dot treatment may be seen on the vessels illustrated herein as Figures 26*b* and 27*b*.

Plain band treatment (Figure 47d-f).—Even plain rim bands can be very diagnostic early Marksville markers when set off by a broad incised line and a row of hemiconical punctates. The plain band treatment is often supplemented by notching along the front edge of the lip.

www.ingramcontent.com/pod-product-compliance
Lightning Source LLC
LaVergne TN
LVHW050022250826
846302LV00008B/58
* 9 7 8 0 9 3 2 2 0 6 5 4 1 *